Kristin Augsburg, Isabell A. Claus,
Kasim Randeree (Eds.)

Leadership and the Emirati Woman

International Economics

Volume 4

LIT

Leadership and the Emirati Woman

Breaking the Glass Ceiling in the Arabian Gulf

edited by

Kristin Augsburg, Isabell A. Claus
and Kasim Randeree

LIT

Printed with support of

RAK FREE TRADE ZONE

Cover Picture: Sheikh Zayed Bin Sultan Al Nahyan Mosque
Photo by Sandra Woest

Bibliographic information published by the Deutsche Nationalbibliothek
The Deutsche Nationalbibliothek lists this publication in the Deutsche Nationalbibliografie; detailed bibliographic data are available in the Internet at http://dnb.d-nb.de.

ISBN 978-3-643-10251-5

A catalogue record for this book is available from the British Library

Fresnostr. 2 D-48159 Münster
Tel. +49 (0) 2 51-620 32 22 Fax +49 (0) 2 51-922 60 99
e-Mail: lit@lit-verlag.de http://www.lit-verlag.de

Distribution:

In Germany: LIT Verlag Fresnostr. 2, D-48159 Münster
Tel. +49 (0) 2 51-620 32 22, Fax +49 (0) 2 51-922 60 99, e-Mail: vertrieb@lit-verlag.de

In Austria: Medienlogistik Pichler-ÖBZ GmbH & Co KG
IZ-NÖ, Süd, Straße 1, Objekt 34, A-2355 Wiener Neudorf
Tel. +43 (0) 22 36-63 53 52 90, Fax +43 (0) 22 36-63 53 52 43, e-Mail: mlo@medien-logistik.at

In Switzerland: B + M Buch- und Medienvertriebs AG
Hochstr. 357, CH-8200 Schaffhausen
Tel. +41 (0) 52-643 54 85, Fax +41 (0) 52-643 54 35, e-Mail: order@buch-medien.ch

Distributed in the UK by: Global Book Marketing, 99B Wallis Rd, London, E9 5LN
Phone: +44 (0) 20 8533 5800 – Fax: +44 (0) 1600 775 663
http://www.centralbooks.co.uk/html

Distributed in North America by:

Transaction Publishers
New Brunswick (U.S.A.) and London (U.K.)

Transaction Publishers
Rutgers University
35 Berrue Circle
Piscataway, NJ 08854

Phone: +1 (732) 445 - 2280
Fax: + 1 (732) 445 - 3138
for orders (U. S. only):
toll free (888) 999 - 6778
e-mail: orders@transactionpub.com

ACKNOWLEDGEMENTS

The authors would like to thank all the women profiled in this book for their time and patience during the interview process. Special thanks go out to the Ras Al Khaimah Freezone Authority and to the German Industry and Commerce Office for their support of the project and to Sandra Woest for the cover picture of the book.

Preface

His Highness, the late Sheikh Zayed bin Sultan Al Nahyan, founder and first president of the United Arab Emirates (UAE) said, *"Nothing could delight me more than to see the woman taking up her distinctive position in society … Nothing should hinder her progress … Like men, women deserve the right to occupy high positions according to their capabilities and qualifications."*

The role of Arab women is often perceived one-sided in Western countries. In fact this perception must be revised when looking at the achievements of women in the United Arab Emirates. The booming economy – one of the fastest growing economies in the world – demands for a well educated society. According to the UAE Yearbook 2007, 16.1 per cent of national women contributed to economic activity in 2004 coming from 3.4 per cent in 1980. A 2005 Forbes list of "Women to Watch in the Middle East" included two Emirati women. Telling the success stories of Emirati women in leadership positions will give exposure to the West and serve to counterpoint existing prejudices about the opportunities for women in the UAE.

TABLE OF CONTENTS

THE UNITED ARAB EMIRATES AT A GLANCE

"Unique, one of its kind, extraordinary, the world's biggest, largest, tallest, most exclusive" – these are words journalists love to use when describing the United Arab Emirates (UAE). Some may find these descriptions exaggerated, sometimes even repetitive. But all criticism and perhaps envy aside – from a very objective point of view, the UAE have had a visibly incredible development over a very short period of time. From a society of nomads and pearl divers, struggling to make a living in an extremely harsh climate, to the most modern and liberal country in the region with a prospering economy with double-digit growth rates, a world-class infrastructure and a politically stable and visionary environment, the UAE have come a very long way.

It was only in 1971 that the emirates of Abu Dhabi, Dubai, Sharjah, Um al Quwain, Fujairah and Ajman got together to form the UAE. Ras al Khaimah joined a few months later. The area was originally known as the "trucial states" after a series of contracts between local tribes and the United Kingdom which aimed at pacifying the region known as the Pirate Coast. From maintaining maritime truce, these contracts developed into giving Britain control over the foreign affairs of the local sheikhdoms, effectively limiting all commercial relations to the United Kingdom unless specifically approved. In return, the United Kingdom offered protection.

When in 1968 the British announced their intention to draw back from the Gulf region, it was Sheikh Zayed bin Sultan Al Nahyan, ruler of the emirate of Abu Dhabi who immediately began consultations with his neighbours to form a union – a concept unique to the Arab world, but the only guarantee for economic and political independence from strong neighbours such as Saudi Arabia and Iran. During the 1960s, life in the emirates was a long way from being glamorous or even close to comfortable. The estimated population at the time of the foundation was 280,000. Although the region had always been a trading hub, the economy depended largely on pearl diving, fishery and date cultivation. The population was poor, life was exceptionally hard. A trip from Abu Dhabi to Al Ain, a mere 160 km, would take seven days, as there were no paved roads until the early 1960s.

The main reason was that it was not until the 1950s that oil was discovered. It took a further decade to export oil – Abu Dhabi started its oil exports in 1962, Dubai followed in 1969 and Sharjah in 1974. It was the black gold that kick started the economic development, fueled by price jumps during the first oil crisis in the early 1970s. And it was due to a fortunate and visionary leadership of the founding fathers of the UAE under the guidance of Sheikh Zayed that this new wealth was put to good use. Even before oil was found, the ruler of Abu Dhabi had spent his own money on developing the infrastructure and on bringing progress to his people. He was also the driving force behind the new constitution which created a political system unlike any other in the Arab world, and the trust in this leadership is reflected in the fact that the ruler of Abu Dhabi is also the President of the UAE. The head of the second-largest emirate Dubai is traditionally the Vice-President and Prime Minister of the UAE. The rulers of the seven emirates, all absolute monarchs, are represented on federal level through the Supreme Council. As a consultative institution and quasi-parliament, the Federal National Council (FNC) reviews proposed legislation. In December 2006, elections were held for the first time, and while 20 members of the FNC are still appointed, 20 are elected by the local population. 22.5% of FNC members are women (one elected, eight appointed).

With the deaths of two of the UAE's founding fathers, Sheikh Zayed bin Sultan Al Nahyan in 2004 and Sheikh Maktoum bin Rashid Al Maktoum in 2006, a new generation has entered the political scene. Sheikh Zayed's son Sheikh Khalifa bin Zayed Al Nahyan is now ruler of Abu Dhabi and President of the UAE, Sheikh Maktoum's brother Sheikh Mohammed bin Rashid Al Maktoum took over as ruler of Dubai and Vice-President and Prime Minister of the UAE. A cabinet reshuffle resulted in the creation of 20 ministries, of which two are led by women.

UAE nationals and in fact also the expatriate population feel very much connected with their leaders. The old Majlis system of governance which allows anyone to present their grievances to the ruler is still very much a part of the political system. The ruling families enjoy the trust, admiration and support of their people, and by any standard their leadership is visionary. Dubai especially has become the embodiment of globalization. With enrichment of its services sector the UAE, with Dubai at the helm of its expedited development, has seen an intense boom in information and communication technology (ICT). Knowing well that the oil reserves on which the country's first boom was based on are soon to run out, the emirate has early on branched out its economy and diversified to tourism, logistics and services. By now, Dubai boasts a large number of different free zones which allow foreign investors full ownership of their businesses. The Dubai International Financial Center aims to turn Dubai into the region's financial capital. Large-scale projects such as the Palm Islands, Dubailand, Ski Dubai and Burj Dubai have put Dubai on the map. The UAE are home to the only two seven-star hotels in the world. Abu Dhabi is now planning the first emission-free city.

The construction boom in particular has attracted many foreigners which today make up around 80% of the population. As neither parties nor trade unions are allowed, there is relatively little unrest even though a majority of foreigners are low-wage workers.

According to the latest Arab World Competitiveness Report of the World Economic Forum, the UAE is the most competitive economy in the Arab World. Its strength lies in the highly-developed infrastructure and the stability of its institutions and political system. Still in need of development is the educational system, with "inadequately educated workforce" and "poor work ethic in national labor force" listed as two of the most problematic factors for doing business by the Global Competitiveness Report 2007-2008. In May 2007, Sheikh Mohammed bin Rashid Al Maktoum announced the establishment of an education fund worth 2 billion USD to help bridge the knowledge gap in the Middle East. Tackling difficulties head-on is what the Prime Minister of the UAE is known for. "Change or you will be changed" was his message to Arab leaders.

THE ROLE OF WOMEN SINCE THE FOUNDING OF THE UNITED ARAB EMIRATES

INTRODUCTION

The population of United Arab Emirates in 2003 was estimated by the United Nations at 2,995,000, which placed it as number 131 in population among the 193 nations of the world. In that year approximately 1% of the population was over 65 years of age, with another 26% of the population under 15 years of age, with an average age of mortality at 64 for males and 73 for females. There were 186 males for every 100 females in the country in 2003. According to the UN, the annual population growth rate for 2000–2005 is 1.94%, with the estimated population for the year 2008 at 4,100,000. Local estimates are a little higher, with 4,76 million inhabitants at the end of 2008. Currently 78% of the population reside in urban areas, with the remaining 22% living a more traditional rural existence. Like much of the developing world, the trend is toward rural habitation, with a resultant decline in traditional Bedouin life.

The Emirates are settled by a diversity of cultural groups. In addition to UAE nationals, there are various Arab groups as well as Iranians, Filipinos, Indians and large numbers of Europeans and Americans. These are all known as expatriates or abbreviated as expats.

The UAE is a loose but supportive federation of seven emirates with each of the seven emirates retaining considerable autonomy over political, economic and financial affairs. This has enabled a variety of different economic policies to be pursued by individual states. Hence whilst Abu Dhabi has focused on developing its extensive energy resources, holding over 90% of the UAE's oil reserves, the other emirates have sought other economic drivers as their oil reserves are relatively limited. Trade has become the UAE's staple. Successful strategies are copied in the other emirates and the resulting increase in competition deepens the market and allows for the spread of best practice.

This process has been supported by the UAE's heavy investment in infrastructure, principally in Dubai, where world class airports and naval ports have been built. Dubai is undergoing a 1.4 billion USD airport ex-

pansion and has an open skies policy which has led to over 100 airlines connecting through Dubai International Airport. However, it has been the establishment of 'free zones' that has led to the UAE being used increasingly as a business hub for the region. These zones grant 100% foreign ownership and exemption from taxes, tariffs and local regulations. Jebel Ali Free Zone (JAFZ), part of the emirate of Dubai, is home to over 6000 companies from over 100 countries, including many European and American blue chip companies. The UAE has been at the forefront of this policy and has moved into creating dedicated industrial or services zones in an effort to attract clusters of leading companies within targeted sectors. The UAE's most recent ambitious project, the Dubai International Financial Centre is the latest and it is hoped that it will support the development of a regional capital market.
In a region that is amongst the most expensive and time consuming to start a business, the UAE's free zones are attractive propositions. Consequently, over the last twenty years, the UAE has become the leading business and trading hub in the Middle East. In other areas, too, the UAE is excelling. Although construction and real estate investment have picked up across the Middle East over the last two years, the UAE has seen the most activity, with investment in Dubai's real estate sector accounting for over 20% of the emirate's GDP.

The UAE's 2010 vision for a K-economy is a strategy for developing the model for growth and development in the region. A K-economy, as defined by the World Bank, rests on 4 pillars, known as "infrastructure", "incentives", "innovation" and "intelligence".

Infrastructure relates to the information society infrastructure and the dissemination and processing of information and how effectively a society gives people access to affordable and effective information and communications. Incentives relate to the economic and institutional framework, providing a stable macro-economy, a competitive environment, a flexible labour market and adequate social protection. Innovation brings together research and business activities in commercial applications of science and technology, with emerging sectors such as pharmaceuticals, bio- and nanotechnologies and wireless communication systems. Finally, intelligence refers to education systems, where citizens acquire, share and use knowledge.

The UAE has set its sights on joining the ranks of the world's leading K-economies with a comprehensive strategy to enhance knowledge-driven development. Dubai in particular, seeks to transform itself into a knowledge-based society and K-economy by the year 2010.

To achieve this objective it has set itself many strategic targets. By 2010, it aims to generate 25% of its GDP from knowledge-based industries and seeks to raise the role of Foreign Direct Investment (FDI) in the country's economy to 4% of the GDP which will play a role in creating job opportunities in the country.

WOMEN IN THE UAE WORKFORCE

The UAE is not without its difficulties, however, as it faces many challenges including future demographics, employment of its national workforce, sustainability issues, educational concerns, as well as diversity and gender problems.

In truth, the active participation of women can help in alleviating many of the UAE's problems. The challenge for its rulers and people of power is to engage women in education and employment whilst still moving in step with advanced nations and respecting Arab and Islamic tradition.

The demographic data of Dubai indicates that it is a unique city in a global context (Table 1). Dubai Municipality's Statistical Yearbook of 2004 states that Dubai had a population of c.1.1 M, under a third of UAE's 3.7 M but covers an area of only 4.9% of the UAE. With a female population of only 27%, significant issues of gender and equality are raised. Population growth is extremely high due to the influx of foreign male expatriate workers and with a growth rate of women at only 3%, issues of sustainability and Emiratisation become prominent. Furthermore, a proportionately high workforce coupled with a reliance on expatriate employees means that issues of working conditions, continuity, transience and stability are raised. Though in 1980 only 8,000 women were employed in Dubai compared to over 60,000 today, employment levels significantly favour men and are disproportionate compared to the West.

The UAE is thus potentially a successful model for change in the Arabian Gulf region, in issues pertaining to the necessity for the full participation of women in the workforce and at managerial level in the developing knowledge based economy.

Middle East economies generally lag behind global competitors in part because the vast resource of female talent remains untapped. There are therefore many challenges facing the Arab world including the United Arab Emirates. However, due to the advancement and comparatively liberal na-

Parameter	*Ratio / %*	*World Rank*
Male to Female Ratio	2.62 male to 1 female	Highest
Workforce to population ratio	68.33%	Highest
Expats as % of population	82.00%	Highest
Population growth	7.00%	Highest
Population over 65 years old	0.65%	Lowest

Table 1: Dubai Demographic World Records (Madar Research Group, 2004)

ture of the UAE in comparison to other countries in the region, the international community looks to the UAE as a model for a new, prosperous and sustainable 21st century Middle East. Attitudes of women are changing.

Young women in the UAE are joining the workforce and the challenges they face are a source of much intrigue in the international media. Furthermore, women in the UAE are diversifying into sectors and activities not traditionally occupied by women. TV presenters, forensic scientists, Dot Com entrepreneurs, medical professionals and taxi drivers are amongst some of the wider professions where women are playing an active role.

The UAE's construction industry too, appears to be more accepting to women in administrative positions and female engineers are often sought. It has become a familiar trend to see women on construction sites performing work that until recent years was labelled as 'a man's job'. This is not to say that women have only started to do a good job, but rather the growing numbers of female professionals has contributed to their recognition. Thus, prejudice can be retracted once female leader's accomplishments and actions are observed.

The emphasis on diversification in the Emirates, especially visible in Dubai, has led to an increased demand of qualified professionals in the services section. In 2004 female employment was predominant in the health care and education services sector and Emirati women in the federal government zone. However, ever since the announcement of the Dubai 2010 Knowledge economy vision in 2005 and the accelerated economic growth across the emirates there is a visible increase in aspiring Emirati women. Companies such as the Ras Al Khaimah Freetrade Zone recall facing some difficulties in the early days of trying to promote employing local women. As there were only few women working in those days, families were sceptical and needed assurance that their daughters would be working in a respected company. They were encouraged to come and visit them at work.

While at first the parents were waiting outside the buildings to pick up their daughters after work, things gradually changed. Nowadays with the trust of the family gained, balancing work and family has shifted to other areas of concern. Companies start offering crèches for their female employers to improve the productivity of female staff in the organisation and reduce the turnover as it removes anxiety of the mother to have to leave their children at home.

While there are a number of projects aiming at supporting young Emirati women on their way into the workforce, almost all of these target women at managerial level. It is worth mentioning a project by the Roads and Transport Authority which established 'pink taxis' on Dubai's roads, taxis driven exclusively by female drivers and only for female customers or families. While not strictly intended to increase the amount of Emirati women in the workforce, it still employs a number of UAE national drivers and thus supports their activities below managerial level.

WOMEN AND THE LEGAL AND POLITICAL SYSTEMS

The polity of the UAE is based on a federation of traditional monarchies, where a president is elected every 5 years. Since the withdrawal of the British and the abandonment of the Trucial States followed by the establishment of the UAE in December 1971, the Ruler of Abu Dhabi has always been appointed president, Shaikh Zayed bin Sultan Al Nahyan, from 1971 until his death in November 2004, followed by his son, Shaikh Khalifa bin Zayed Al Nahyan, to the present day.

The legal system of the UAE is based on a dual court system, with a Sharia court for oversight in criminal law and a secular court for civil cases. Non-Muslims have trials in Sharia court for criminal offenses, but judges frequently discharge a civil penalty for proven offenders. In the legal system, a woman is considered a full person and adult at the age of 18.

Women's rights and legal status in the UAE depends largely on her residency and employment status. She may fall into one of four categories, a UAE citizen, a professional foreign worker on a time constrained employment visa, another foreign worker, such as domestic help, maids etc or a wife of a foreign worker.

The rights of women in law and their political participation are largely consistent with conservative Islamic nations, with the UAE holding an UN Human Development Index rating of 49 out of 177 countries. Published ratings on the freedom women have to exercise their rights have placed the

UAE similarly to other GCC nations. On a scale of 1-5, with 1 being low on an assessment of women's rights, in terms of non-discrimination and access to justice, the UAE scored 1.7; the ability of women to exercise their personal freedom, have autonomy in decision making and security (2.1); the right to economic advancement and equality of opportunity (2.8); political rights and an ability to exercise their voice within civil society (1.2); rights within a social and cultural context (2.3). These statistics are consistent with other data. For example, the relatively high score in economic rights is supported by the fact that over 32% of women are economically active and that the UAE has one of the highest per capita GDP in the world, 22,420 USD. Women are allowed to own, license and head businesses. However, rights to non discrimination and access to justice score low, in part because of exploitation of women. For example, the federal law of 1996 outlaws the trafficking of women for labour or sexual exploitation. Nevertheless, the practice does continue within the UAE, largely from Asia and former Soviet republics, despite government attempts to curtail trafficking by limiting entry for single women and banning women from Soviet republics under the age of 30.

In family law, the UAE determines inheritance based on the religion of the deceased. Sharia law, contrary to civil law as practiced in Western countries, is based on the principle that provision is made for women on the basis of them being supported by men, thus an unequal share is given.

Similarly, UAE male citizens are provided housing either by donating a piece of land to them upon which they can build, or by giving a cash sum of 500,000 Dirhams or by providing a previously built house. Women, on the other hand, are given no such allowance, with the expectation that she will be housed by her husband or another male relative.

Politically, the UAE has no political parties and has limited rights of assembly for its population. Dissent against the ruling families is therefore not tolerated. Non-governmental organisations are required to register with the authorities and always have the threat of closure without notice. There are no trade unions to represent the vast expatriate labour market and, consequently, limited or no protection. No independent human rights organisations work in the country to assess possible violations.

In employment law, Articles 27 and 28 of UAE Labour Law, published by the UAE Ministry of Labour and Social Affairs in 1980, stipulates that women are not required to work nights between the hours of 10 pm and 7 am, nor do they have to do dangerous or arduous work or work detrimental to health or morals. It can also be said that in addition to male stereotyping of women, the self image amongst many Arab women of inferiority to men is potentially a more harmful obstacle to professional achievement.

For its part, the federal government has facilitated this activity by enshrining its support for women and their rights in the workplace into law. UAE Labour Law thus ensures that a woman's remuneration is equal to that of a man's if she performs the same work, that she receive 45 days maternity leave with full pay and even allows breaks for breastfeeding, or leaving work one hour early for 18 months post partum. UAE law stipulates that a foreign woman be granted citizenship if she marries a UAE citizen. However, this law does not apply in reverse, thus a female UAE citizen marrying a foreign national does not grant the husband citizenship rights.

Further, a law passed in 1996 requires Emirati women to surrender their citizenship when marrying a non-GCC citizen, with exclusion only by presidential approval. In 1992, to curb the rising trend of male UAE citizens marrying foreign women, the government endorsed a marriage fund to encourage men to marry citizens from the UAE. In laws relating to custody of children after divorce, custody is granted to the mother until maturity in the case of girls and until the age of 13 in the case of boys. However, a mother revokes her right to custody of children from a previous marriage, were she to remarry.

EDUCATION FOR WOMEN

The education system in the UAE is based on a segregated gender policy for all state owned schools and universities. The system has, in the past, been considered as coherent with the development of individuals within the nation, as women have traditionally gone on to work in segregated public sector work. The proportionately large number of university female students is accounted for by the fact that, contrary to men, women are not encouraged to seek higher education abroad. As the nation faces transformations and accelerated growth, the education system is coming under careful analysis.

The UAE experienced major challenges during its process of nation building and economic development. A major uncertainty during the process was the training and development of national human resources to enable them to take an active role in supporting and contributing towards the country's rapid development. This was a complex task and indeed a huge challenge given that until 1962, when oil production started in Abu Dhabi, the country had just 20 schools for less than 4,000 students, most of them boys. However this has been changed and developed dramatically by introducing the government and private education with different educational levels and experiences.

Thus, the UAE has enshrined for men and women, both in its Constitution and through the commitment of the rulers of the various Emirates, the rights and opportunities for education for all its citizens. Education has become imperative in the acquisition of a higher standard of living. Furthermore, according to the World Economic Forum, access to education is one of the primary indicators of women's status and is the root of women's emancipation.

Although the UAE has the second highest GDP in the Gulf, it is lowest in terms of percentage GDP spent on education. However, the number of girls completing secondary education is 88% and 69% of Emirati graduates are women. Furthermore, according to World Bank statistics, female illiteracy dropped from 29% to 21% between 1990 and 2000, whereas male illiteracy only dropped from 29% to 25% during the same period. The educational level in the county also plays an important role in shaping the capabilities of UAE nationals to be able to compete in the workplace.

Education is a national priority, especially in the light of technological revolutions and scientific advancement witnessed by the entire world which could only be encountered by a well-developed and effective educational system.

To address this disparate composition of the workforce, many of the Gulf Cooperation Council (GCC) countries embarked on training and development programs in order to promote the employment of nationals in the labour market. This was accompanied by the government-mandated Emiratisation policy, mechanisms to stem the inflow of foreign workers and encouragement of the employment of UAE nationals. Measures to control the growth of foreign workers typically included mandated targets for Emiratisation in the private sectors, permit requirements and levy for foreign workers and attractive incentives and preferential treatment for companies adhering to nationalisation policies.

Owing to the rapid development of economy in various sectors that required skilled labour resulted in creation of additional educational institutions and training centers. One of the important colleges that provide the market with qualified and skilled graduates that are able to handle the jobs is Higher Colleges of Technology. Furthermore, Tanmia has established the Employment and Skills Development Center (ESDC), which had an agreement with UAE University to create a link between the job seekers and the employers. Also, the Continuing Education Center of the UAE University trains the jobseekers that are listed in Tanmia with the latest technology and skills needed in the market at subsidised prices. Tanmia was created by the Government to assist UAE nationals in finding jobs. Its main function is to organize and match the employers with the jobseekers and the skills they have. So, basically employers list vacant positions and the criteria they require, and Tanmia finds the equivalent skills that would fit their requirements after running through the list of jobseekers submitted. As part of their aim to advance the percentage of nationals in the workforce, Tanmia created a website that allows jobseekers to apply online and search for employers of their choice. Not only that, the website also allows employers to search for candidates for vacant positions.

Expedited growth in the private sector compared to the public sector and the emphasis on Emiratisation has created a huge demand for labour force and encouraged the private sector to recruit and train nationals.

The experience of Emirati national development and economic growth is similar to neighbouring GCC countries. The distinctiveness of the Emirati experience lies in its history as a developing country. The UAE shares similar constraints with the other GCC countries in terms of availability of educated and experienced local workforce. According to the MERIP Reports published in 1975, the socio-political and economic circumstances of UAE during most of the twentieth century, coupled with the lack of modern educational facilities prior to 1971, has resulted in its under-development as well as a shortage of educated citizens. This predicament affects all sectors but is particularly acute in the private sector.

YOUNG WOMEN IN EMIRATI SOCIETY

The hopes and aspirations of young Emirati women are changing. Recent studies have demonstrated a marked change in their views on personal expectations and values, attitudes, family, marriage and employment. A survey amongst female Emirati university students in the UAE, conducted by the American University in Sharjah, demonstrated that only 1% of them planned to stay at home after graduation, whereas 65% of them planned to work. Over half of them expressed a wish to work for the government of their respective emirate, with only 42% wanting to enter the private sector. This is largely due to the fact that government sector work times and benefits are very favourable towards Emirati citizens. The work is viewed as significantly less demanding than in the private sector and families are more willing for their daughters to work in this sector rather than in the private sector. A significant proportion of those interviewed (one quarter) were of the view that the 'Wasta' system (exercising tribal and other influences) was most likely to facilitate them into a desirable position. Fewer thought that their university major would have bearing on them getting a job.

Women's views on marriage are changing too. The average age of an Emirati woman marrying in the 1980's was 18. Emirati women now aspire to marry much later in their lives, with women typically indicating mid to late twenties as being appropriate. Only one fifth of university graduates planned to marry after their studies, rising to one third within the first five years of graduation.

According to UNICEF, only 28% of women in the age group 15-49 use contraception, though this low figure is largely explained by the fact that non-marital relations are disapproved of in broader society and the use of birth control pills within marriage is taboo. There are no reported cases of abortion, which was declared illegal in penal code in 1975, except in life threatening circumstances, though doctors practicing illegal abortion have been imprisoned in the past. Women do however express the desire to have fewer children than previous generations. This determination is bourne out by the data too, with 5.3 children per child bearing woman in 1980-1985 against only 3 children by the year 2000. However, young women do favour balancing a family life with a career, rather than remaining single, with 65% of women believing that an education and career is no barrier to getting married and starting a family. Attitudes towards the cultural and religious practice of polygamy are changing significantly. Four fifths of women would not consider it acceptable for her husband to marry a second wife and over two thirds would prefer to remain a spinster rather than being in a polygamous relationship.

ROLE MODELS OF A NATION

It is important for women in the Middle East including Emirati women to have role models in order to encourage them, as well as their families into understanding that their participation in society is desirable and welcome. Though female historical figures have existed throughout the history of Arab and Islamic civilisation, living personalities have only recently become familiar.

HER HIGHNESS SHEIKHA FATIMA BINT MUBARAK

The "mother of the nation" as Her Highness Sheikha Fatima bint Mubarak is frequently refered to, is a key person for the development of women in the UAE and an internationally active agent for women's rights.

Born in Al Hayer in Al Ain city as the only daughter to her parents, H. H. Sheikha Fatima bint Mubarak Al Ketbi was married to H. H. Sheikh Zayed bin Sultan Al Nahyan, President of the UAE, during the 1960s when he was ruler of the Eastern region. H. H. Sheikha Fatima moved to Abu Dhabi when H. H. Sheikh Zayed seized the rule of the Emirate of Abu Dhabi on 16th August 1966. H. H. Sheikha Fatima is an example for a woman in her standing with her husband in all circumstances in bringing up their children, preserving her religious and traditional principles, having prudence and insight and interacting with all modern development chosen for the environment and society.

H.H. Sheikha Fatima is the mother of Their Highnesses Mohammed bin Zayed, Hamdan, Hazzaa, Tahnoun, Mansour, Abdullah, Shamaa and Alyazia Al Nahyan.

H. H. Sheikha Fatima, encouraged by her husband H. H. Sheikh Zayed, contributed outstandingly to the development of women nationally in the UAE, regionally in the Middle East and internationally. Just to name a few examples of her current posts, H. H. Sheikha Fatima is the Chairwoman of the UAE's Family Development Foundation, the UAE General Women's Union (GWU) and the Cairo-based Arab Women's Organisation (AWO).

Looking back, H. H. Sheikha Fatima initiated the establishment of the first women's organization in the UAE in 1973 called the Abu Dhabi Women Development Society. It was established as the first women's assembly in the country. H. H. Sheikha Fatima set up the initial basics for great achievements of the Emirati women after the declaration of the UAE's foundation on the 2nd of December 1971. The business activities of local women have received much importance since the women sector represents the second half of the society as being in charge with bringing up the new generations and achieving the national dream of the modern state. Consequently, H. H. Sheikha Fatima opened her sitting hall to meet her country's women and she participates with them in building the modern state following the steps of H. H. Sheikh Zayed in the constructional march in which both men and women cooperate to develop their country. At the same time, it was H. H. Sheikha Fatima too, who started the first nation-wide campaigns of educating young girls as she considered illiteracy to be the first obstacle in the way to progress. And it was H. H. Sheikha Fatima too, who in 1975 initiated the establishment of the UAE Women's Federation to assist in developing the image and self-esteem of women, to encourage education and to eradicate illiteracy among adult women, to ensure that social services and care reached the needy women and their families, to plan activities to raise cultural standards and to build links with women's organizations internationally. The Federation was the first official women's gathering which acted on the international scene and it participated in international conferences, for example in the first women summit in Mexico City right after the federation's founding in 1975.

Through the organizations and committees for women H. H. Sheikha Fatima could meet the women of the Emirate of Abu Dhabi and encourage them to prepare themselves in order to be able to fulfill their missions toward the nation, the society and the family. With the help of networking and visionary inspiration H. H. Sheikha Fatima aimed to support women in their development to achieve their maximum potential. After primary education needs in the country were satisfied to an acceptable level, H. H. Sheikha Fatima saw women achieving much more and developing far beyond. Examples of her campaigns that opened doors for careers of women in the private as well as the public sector include initiatives for the women of the UAE to work in the media or to become members of the country's parliamentary assembly, the Federal National Council (FNC). In 2003 H. H. Sheikha Fatima recommended meetings between the FNC and the General Women's Union (GWU) which she heads to allow the two sides to debate the vital issue and establish strong links of cooperation and coordination before a high-level decision is taken to approve female membership in the FNC. A series of meeting took place and finally in 2006 her dreams bore fruits. Mrs. Amal Al-Qaisi became the first elected female member of the Federal National Council. Moreover the rulers of the various emirates appointed eight other women to the FNC as part of their jurisdiction to nominate 20 appointed members. According to an interview with H. H. Sheikha Fatima in 2008 taken from "UAE Interact", she sees this achievement of women as the most visible one in the country.

"Among the most visible gains for UAE women are a greater number of seats in the Cabinet formed in February 2008 and in the Federal National Council. There are now four women in the Cabinet, compared to two previously, the largest number in the Arab world, and 9 out of 40 FNC seats, or 22 per cent, which is among the highest anywhere in the world's legislative bodies."

And as H. H. Sheikha Fatima points out in the interview taken from "UAE Interact", there are women becoming successful in many other areas:

"H.H. Sheikh Khalifa, in his capacity as Ruler of Abu Dhabi, has also appointed Kholoud Jua'an Al Dhahiri as the first-ever female judge in the UAE. She was sworn in on October 7th 2008 before H.H. Sheikh Mansour bin Zayed Al Nahyan, Minister of Presidential Affairs and Chairman of the Abu Dhabi Judicial Department. This appointment was an example of the continuation of the policy of engaging women in the overall process of development and encouraging them to work in all areas alongside men on an equal opportunity basis. Sheikha Najla Al Qassimi and Dr. Hussa Al Otaiba were also recently named as the first two Emirati female ambassadors in the UAE's history, being appointed to Sweden and Spain respectively."

Not only individual examples can be named when describing the development of Emirati women. Statistics of the UAE present a pleasant picture too. Taken from "UAE Interact" H. H. Sheikha Fatima said in an interview in 2008:

"UAE women have become major and active players in the process of development in the UAE. They now account for 66% of the governmental workforce and hold 30% of senior jobs at the decision-making level. They also account for 15% of the teaching staff at the UAE University. In addition, they account for 60% of the workforce in medical care, education, nursing and pharmacies. They have also joined the Armed Forces, police and customs. Following the establishment of the Businesswomen's Council, they have also begun to make their mark in business. The Council now had 12,000 members, managing 11,000 investments estimated at 12.5 billion UAE dirhams. Women now account for 37.5% of the workforce in the banking sector which is one of the pillars of the UAE economy."

Apart from her national activities, H. H. Sheikha Fatima became active outside the UAE too. Regionally and internationally she worked tirelessly. She supported the people in Palestine, in Kosovo and in Iraq to name but a few of her regional focusses. According to an RCS official, the combined value of charity and humanitarian projects implemented by the UAE Red Crescent Society (RCS) on the sponsorship of H. H. Sheikha Fatima have touched Dirham 71.5 million.

As might be expected the achievements of H. H. Sheikha Fatima for women were recognized with numerous highly renowned awards worldwide. In 1997, she was honoured simultaneously by five organizations of the United Nations. These included citations and awards by the United Nations Children's Fund (UNICEF), the World Health Organization (WHO), the United Nations Population Fund (UNFPA), the United Nations Volunteers Program (UNVP), and the United Nations Development Fund for Women (UNIFEM). In fact, UNIFEM described her as a 'Champion of Women's Rights' and praised her 'untiring work to bring about social justice', acknowledging her 'for her tremendous efforts in putting women on the path of gaining access and participation in the political and economic institutions'. H. H. Sheikha Fatima became the third international figure and the first Arab personality to be bestowed with the Marie Curie Medal from the United Nations Educational, Culture and Science (UNESCO) organization in appreciation of her great efforts in the field of education and emancipation of illiteracy and in encouraging women to get involved in various national activities. In appreciation of H. H. Sheikha Fatima's leadership and continuous support for the voluntary works she also received the United Nations Volunteers Program (UNVP) shield. In 2003 in Egypt, H.E. Hussni Mubarak granted for H. H. Sheikha Fatima the Excellent Medal of Perfection, a most renowned medal granted for kings' and presidents' spouses. In 2005, H. H. Sheikha Fatima has also been selected by a Moroccan paper as one of the most outstanding female personalities who made a great contribution to humanity. The Moroccan Desert newspaper noted that "H.H. Sheikha Fatima has demonstrated lofty humane gestures in every endeavour she had pursued", citing her important role in promoting community services and preserving family traditions. In 2006, she was also awarded with the prestigious French decoration, Chevalier dans l'Ordre des Palmes Académiques, a decoration instituted by Napoleon in 1808, to recognize outstanding efforts in education, culture, and education research. The award was given in appreciation of her pioneering role in support of women's causes at local, regional and international levels. The highest international honour and recognition came in 2007 when the United Nations honoured H. H. Sheikha Fatima in recognition of her outstanding contributions to women's empowerment in the UAE. The decision to honour her came after the Security Council called on member states and the Secretary-General to bolster efforts to empower women and increase their representation in decision-making reasserting how crucial women are in preventing and resolving conflicts and in peace building.

H. H. Sheikha Fatima does not lay back and enjoy what is achieved. Instead she makes further plans and has her clear vision of what is essential to the development of women in her country and elsewhere. She said in an interview in 2008 taken from "UAE Interact":

"We live in a global age ... Economic security is determined by global, regional, local and national factors. Arab countries are going through a lot of economic changes and have already adopted a market economy. The impacts of these changes on women are different than those on men."

In the interview she also names one of the channels most important to support women's development.

"The greatest responsibility for supporting and encouraging the development of Arab women rests on the shoulders of the media. However, Arab women themselves have to take up the opportunities made available to them in the media. A number of factors affect the process of strengthening the presence and role of Arab women in the media."

HER HIGHNESS SHEIKHA LUBNA AL QASIMI

One of the most highly renowned role models for Emirati women is Her Highness Sheikha Lubna Al Qasimi, UAE's Minister of Foreign Trade (appointed in 2008) and former Minister of Economy and Planning (2004-2008) and the first female UAE minister.

H. H. Sheikha Lubna is a member of the ruling family of the Emirate of Sharjah and the niece to H. H. Dr. Sheikh Sultan bin Mohammed Al Qassimi. It is the members of her family that she names first in the list of role models for her own life. Quoting from an interview in 2000 with "Women One", she said:

"What I have become is a by-product of both their personalities (mother and father) ... if I sit there with a psychologist he will tell you, 'This is what she got from her father. This is what she got from her mother'. And I see it today – the discipline, the initiatives, the pride of myself as a woman comes from my mum. But then, loving the world and the creativity – that's from my dad ... My uncle – he really believes in education ... because of him, young girls can actually travel abroad and get an education. To him, the quality of an individual is his education."

H. H. Sheikha Lubna graduated from the California State University, Chico with a Bachelor's Degree in Computer Science, and she graduated from the American University of Sharjah with an Executive MBA. Quoting an interview with "Women One" of 2000 it becomes clear that the inspiration for achieving what she achieved until today came out of herself:

"Since I was at the age of 9 and 10, I always had this in my head that I wanted to have a path of my own. When I decided to go to school and go for computer science, I was just 17 years and lived a sheltered, very over-protected life. But there was always this eagerness that I really wanted to do something."

When H. H. Sheikha Lubna returned to the UAE she did not work in the public sector but started as a programmer for a software company right away. Her boss – with an Indian nationality – was one of the people in her life that taught her what discipline in her job means. Quoting from an interview in 2008 with "The Spiegel" she said:

"I was the only woman, the only Arab, and the only princess at his firm. I earned a thousand dollars a month – and he taught me what discipline is. One time there was a problem with the bookkeeping software. "I'll take care of it tomorrow," I told my boss. "No," he answered, "you'll do it today. There are 2,000 people waiting for their wages."

Later she acted as the Dubai branch manager for the General Information Authority, an organization responsible for automation in the UAE federal government administration before she took up the position of a senior manager of the Information Systems department at the Dubai Ports Authority (DPA), the largest port in the Middle East. It was in this position when H. H. Sheikha Lubna was awarded with the "Distinguished Government Employee Award" in 1999 and attracted the attention of His Highness Sheikh Mohammed bin Rashid Al Maktoum, Ruler of Dubai and Chairman of Dubai Ports and Customs. Today she summarizes her experiences at DPA as follows, quoting from an interview in 2008 with "ETurboNews":

"Sending solutions that rely heavily upon technology as its backbone, the DPA has furnished me with a solid ground. It was my university in terms of learning and acquiring business opportunities."

After seven years at DPA she was appointed as Chief Executive of Tejari, the first Middle Eastern Business-to-Business marketplace. She describes her duties at Tejari as follows, quoting from an interview in 2008 with "ETurboNews":

"Tejari.com allowed me to collaborate technology with business ventures, mastering it to a level of new services and ventures … Within only 60 days, my task was to establish the company, to recruit people, to develop the exchange itself and have it up and running. We were to be ready on the 20th of June, the launch date. Indeed in 60 days, we were demonstrating live transactions on the market that gained for us widespread confidence in the region. It has been a phenomenal achievement to be able to demonstrate tremendous visibility in the market as a dot-com, as new, up and coming company at the marketplace in such a short time. We aim to build a strategy to capture the world's attention through the valuable e-commerce services and e-business opportunities we offer the region especially in Dubai while taking a ride on the net economy."

Under H. H. Sheikha Lubna's leadership, Tejari won the awards for the World Summit for Information Society's "Best e-Content Provider in e-business" (Geneva) and the UAE Super Brands Council's "Super Brand of 2003".

These accomplishments drew the attention of the then-deputy leader of Dubai, H. H. Sheikh Mohammed bin Rashid Al Maktoum, who actively promoted the political career of H. H. Sheikha Lubna. In 2004, she was nominated to the prestigious post of Minister of Economy and Housing – one of very few female ministers of economy worldwide, and the first female UAE minister. In 2008, in a cabinet reshuffle that brought the number of women in high-ranking ministerial posts from two to four, H. H. Sheikha Lubna was nominated as Minister of Foreign Trade.

Today H. H. Sheikha Lubna – besides her duty as the Minister of Foreign Trade – sits on a number of boards in organizations nationally and internationally, such as on the Board of Directors for Dubai Chamber of Commerce & Industry, Board of Trustees for Dubai University College, Board of Trustees for Electronic-Total Quality Management College, Dubai, Board of Trustees for Thunderbird School of Global Management, Glendale, Arizona, USA, Board of Trustees for Zayed University, Board of Directors for the Dubai Autism Center, Board of Directors for Simsari.com, Board of Directors (Honorary) for National U.S.-Arab Chamber of Commerce.

She also got a number of awards in her career, such as the "Dubai Quality Group – for Support to Leadership" award, the "Quality, and Change" award, the "ITP Best Personal Achievement Award", the "Datamatix IT Woman of the Year 2001" award, the "Business. Com Personal Contribution Award", the "Datamatix Outstanding Contribution" award, the "Commonwealth of Kentucky Honorary title – Kentucky Colonel" or the "World Summit Award for Tejari.com".

Significantly, H. H. Sheikha Lubna was included in the Forbes's "Women to Watch in the Middle East" list in 2005 about which she stated:

"I hope my inclusion on the 'Women to Watch' list provides encouragement and inspiration for women across the UAE who are considering a professional career."

However at the end it is not the awards that honour her most. In fact it is the recognition that she receives from local men in the UAE. Quoting from an interview in 2000 with "WomenOne" she said:

"I have met a lot of local men at conferences in Abu Dhabi and Dubai and also this conference in New York and the UK … and I get emails saying 'for us it

is such a pride to be sitting there listening to you thinking this is a UAE woman talking'. For me, that is the biggest credit I have received so far and these are local, national men in the society. And to me that is the best honour … that they will take the liberty of sending this email saying that or come directly to tell me 'well done… we are so proud… you are a pride to us in the UAE'. That is my highest recognition."

Besides all her outstanding achievements and hard work, H. H. Sheikha Lubna is fully aware of the important role she plays for women – and men – in the UAE society and uses every opportunity to spread her knowledge and inspiration to others whenever possible for her. Quoting an interview in 2007 with CNN she said:

"In my personal belief you need a bridge, you need a door opener for women. And sometimes women do not want to take the risk. Sometimes they are shy of achieving what they should be achieving. I had the opportunity and I had the trust from the government and the community, so to me, it is setting the example internally for the young women, and men by the way. Be it in technology, or economy or e-commerce."

WOMEN IN POLITICS

Women are taking a keener interest in the politics of their nation. It started to become visible in 2002 when H. H.Sheikh Sultan Al Qassimi, the Ruler of Sharjah appointed five women to his consultative council. Later, in 2004, H. H. Sheikha Lubna – as explained above – became the first female minister (Minister of Economy and Planning) in the UAE federal government. In 2006 Mariam Mohammed Khalfan Al Roumi followed her as the Minister of Social Affairs. She was born in 1957 and holds a BA in English Literature from the UAE University. Before joining the government she acted as Under Secretary of the Labour and Social Affairs Ministry since 1999. In 2008 the number of female ministers was raised to four. Dr Maitha Al-Shamsi joined as Minister of State. She obtained a PhD in Sociology from Ain Shams University in Egypt in 1992. She held the post of deputy director of the UAE University for Scientific Research and Director of the university's Centre for Research and Foreign Consultations and was also the Chairperson of the Scientific Research Board of the UAE University. Also Reem Al-Hashimy was sworn in as a Minister of State. In addition to her Ministerial duties, she also manages the External Affairs Unit of The Executive Office (TEO) of H. H. Sheikh Mohammed Bin Rashid Al Maktoum.

In the Federal National Council (FNC) elections of December 2006, another 65 of the 439 candidates across all the seven emirates were women. H.H. Sheikh Mohammed bin Rashid Al Maktoum, Vice President and Prime Minister of the UAE and ruler of Dubai, stated in 2006:

"The active participation of women in the elections is a natural extension of her role in the society and the family."

Amal Abdullah Al Qubaisi, a British-educated professor of architecture at the Emirates University, won a seat in Abu Dhabi, becoming the first woman member of the FNC. She won the third highest number of votes in Abu Dhabi. She is fully aware that her success walked hand in hand with Sheikha Fatima's achievements for women in the UAE. At the Second Conference of GCC Women Parliamentarians she said in 2007:

"Her Highness Sheikha Fatima's prediction about women in the FNC was considered an impossible goal back then. Today, women's representation at FNC has reached around 23 per cent, one of the highest in the world. The clear vision and unconditional motivation of Her Highness Sheikha Fatima have empowered women and enabled them to emerge as effective parliamentarians and even represent the UAE in overseas forums."

Najla Al Awadi, one of the eight women appointed to the FNC added in an interview in 2007 with "Gulfnews":

"It was a new experience for women in politics. We haven't got the opportunity to educate ourselves about the political participation. We aspire for a more active role for women."

And Political Science assistant professor at the UAE University, Maryam Sultan Lootah, said in an interview in 2007 with "Gulfnews":

"This has given women a push to participate more in society and has assured women that if they can be at the highest level in the FNC, they can participate in all fields. The presence of women in the FNC really charged women with greater public participation."

Though the FNC's powers remain solely advisory, the move demonstrates a willingness of the government toward political inclusion of women, albeit in a limited representative capacity. Consequently, the United Nations Development Programme (UNDP) stated in its HR report for 2007-08, that the UAE is ahead of USA, UK, France and Canada in regard to women representation in parliament and is the leading Arab country in the parliamentary representation of women. Women in the FNC represent 22.5 per cent of total number of members of parliament.

WOMEN IN THE JUDICIAL SYSTEM

In 2004, women were also appointed to the Judicial Academy as well as in the Ministry of Justice. In early 2008, Abu Dhabi Judicial Department appointed two women as public prosecutors, the first women in the UAE to be hired to this position. Aleya Saeed Al Qaabi and Atiqqah Awad Al Qatheeri graduated from UAE University at the top of their class in 2003, and continued their studies at the Judicial Studies Academy, both completing their coursework in 2006 with top grades. Aleya Saeed Al Qaabi then underwent intensive training in Abu Dhabi's courts and worked as a senior advocate in State cases, while Atiqqah Awad Al Qatheeri spent a year in Al Ain plenary courts and public prosecution office working with the investigations unit. Atiqqah Awad Al Qatheeri said in an interview published by the Abu Dhabi Judicial Department in 2008:

"My family and friends think I am intimidated by my job. Perhaps a little, but it isn't my job that intimidates me-rather, it is the responsibility comes with this position and the high degree of confidence that H.H. Sheikh Khalifa has in us. But I am determined to go the extra mile."

Later in 2008, Khulood Ahmed Jawan Al Dhaheri was appointed the first female judge. At her appointment, she said:

"The decision to appoint female judges helps consolidate UAE women's growing role in public life."

EMIRATISATION AND EMPLOYMENT

Emiratisation is a development that seeks to replace a reliance on foreign expatriate workers with Emirati citizens or nationals in the UAE. To date this has been largely accomplished through various employment quota targets. Expatriate labour accounts for nearly 80% of the workforce in the UAE, with over 50% being Indian men. This is largely due to the fact that these workers undertake work that the native population would be unwilling to do. Even so, the reliance on expatriate males rather than the utilisation of native females means that the gender gap continues to grow. However, the scarcity of a native male population can enhance women's opportunities in an effort to hasten Emiratisation. Local laws and regulations give Gulf employers extensive power over their expatriate employees, often to the detriment of the rights of their employees. While everyone is exposed to such practices, illiterate and unskilled workers from South Asia and the Far

East, with poor understanding of their statutory rights, are the most likely victims.

In the GCC countries, rapid development financed by oil revenues resulted in robust economic growth, infrastructure development and the expansion of public goods provisions. In order to support and sustain this growth in the wake of a shortage of supply of native labour, foreign workers, primarily from the Indian sub-continent, were imported to fulfill this role. Over time, many of the GCC countries became dependent on cheaper and more qualified expatriate labour. In addition, expatriates generally work longer hours, accept lower wages, and tolerate poorer working conditions and more physically demanding jobs as opposed to UAE nationals. Consequently, in most of the GCC countries, over 60% of the labour force are foreign.

Emiratisation is not only recruiting UAE nationals to replace expatriates, it is a major process that requires training these nationals to acquire the skills and competencies for the assigned work, to ensure a successful Emiratisation process. According to the Ministry of Labour, the process of Emiratisation has been quite successful in government and banking sectors. Decisions taken by the Ministry of Labour such as Emiratision of HR management positions before the end of 2008, reflects the seriousness of the government with respect to the process of Emiratisation. Additionally, the financial penalty incurred for organisations lagging behind the target rate of Emiratisation would be utilised for training and development programmes for Emirati nationals.

Emiratisation as a concept does have forces working to its detriment. Most notable is economic migration, the high rate at which expatriate workers continue to flow into the country, largely because of more attractive employment opportunities, better standards of living and higher incomes, as well as better healthcare and educational services for themselves and their families, which are to be found in the UAE.

In terms of Emirati employment, government sector jobs are considered most favourable to most Emiratis. Compared to the private sector, salaries are generally higher, non-monetary benefits are better and hours of work tend to be shorter. Many private sector establishments operate on 10-hour days, six days per week, with a split shift day. In contrast, the government sector operates on a single-shift, eight-hour-day, and five-day-week system.

The Ministry of Labour is making every effort to impose rules and regulations to force the private sector to employ Emirati nationals. Although the majority of the female graduates believe that there is more growth in the private sector, they also see the other side of the coin and sometimes call the private sector 'a no life sector' owing to reasons such as difficulty in managing social life they due to long working hours, more demanding working conditions and pressure.

Women mainly worked in the education and health sectors due to tradition, culture and short working hours. However, with the change in the society's culture and modified rules in the private sector, such as the establishment of the pension scheme in 1999 and providing two days weekend, women's roles in the private sector became more noticeable. Even though there is growth in the government sector, it is not realized as much as it is in the private sector. Subsequently, the Department of Civil Aviation is an example for change in structure to enhance performance, have clear ownerships and responsibilities, and to give employees more opportunities to grow.

However, as society expands ever further and the private sector flourishes, there is now greater urgency to find alternative ways of addressing Emiratisation issues. Among these is the gradual replacement of expatriates with nationals though greater private sector employment of nationals. This, however, presents a dual problem. Firstly, private sector employers have negative perceptions of nationals as less productive than expatriates and so are sometimes unwilling to employ them, despite the fact that ownership of any private establishment must be 51% owned by an Emirati. Secondly, Emirati nationals are legislated to higher salaries than expatriates for the same work, which translate into higher costs for firms. Furthermore, nationals themselves are reluctant to take private sector employment for several reasons. Among these are the perception of lower private sector salaries and benefits compared to the government sector. Other issues include religious observance, translating into the need for nationals to be afforded greater flexibility in working hours. Though legislation has been developed restricting immigration, it is likely that the demographic imbalance between Emirati and expatriate work force will continue to expand for the foreseeable future, so long as the UAE continues to develop and expand its infrastructure. Contribution of women has become much more effective in the labour market adding to the success of the economy.

BUSINESS WOMEN IN ISLAM AND PARTICIPATION OF THE CONTEMPORARY EMIRATI WOMAN

HISTORICAL ROLE OF ARAB AND MUSLIM WOMEN IN COMMERCE

Women's participation within civil society has evolved through Gulf Arab history. During the pre-Islamic era up to approximately 1900, Arab society was generally characterised by tribal disputes and the appropriation of water wells and grazing land as well as herding camels. These activities clearly favour male physical abilities.

From about 1500-1940, an expansion of trade with Europe and Asia was witnessed and seafaring and pearling began. All of these activities were viewed as being incompatible with Islamic tradition in relation to female participation. These new trade links and commercial activities resulted in a movement to coastal inhabitation. Bedouin values of family, honour, chastity and the seclusion of women dominated. Participation of women in Arabian Gulf society outside household duties only went as far as agricultural activities, in so much as maintaining date palms and other agricultural produce as well as livestock, particularly during the absence of male members of the family that were away for several months on fishing and pearling expeditions.

Historically, therefore, the participation of women outside of domestic duties in the Arabian Gulf society was very limited in the pre-oil era. During the 1940's, following the discovery of oil, the first signs of affluence in society within the Arabian Gulf region emerged. This gave rise to education of women which began in earnest in Kuwait in 1937 and in Qatar in 1956. However, it was only after its formation in 1971 that the UAE began educational programmes which included women. Though oil wealth brought prosperity, the absence of economic necessity meant households continued to be supported by the man. Thus, women had an opportunity for education but were still denied participation in the workforce outside of healthcare and educational services.

Around 1990, the emergence of the knowledge-based economy in the Arabian Gulf, characterised by a number of well educated women, lower illiteracy rate, access to global information on women in other societies, non-hierarchical organisational structures and the appearance of women in corporate leadership positions has led to a liberalisation of views in the UAE. In recent years, this liberalisation of attitudes in the UAE society has coincided with women being well educated and this has led to the demand for equality of opportunity in employment. Furthermore, growth in the knowledge economy and the drive for Emiratisation (a policy for reducing the demand for expatriate workers) has led to a need to utilise the female human resource. In the foreseeable future, reduced bureaucratic organisational structures in multinational corporations will lead to a broader participation of all employees in decision making and change. Women are well suited to the new post-contingency flat flexible organisational structure and demonstrate many qualities suited for the economy of the future. The emergence of a host of female Emirati role models within Emirati society is testament to that.

There are numerous myths which are associated with the role of women in organisations. Although stereotyping of women has been around through history and many are untrue, it is particularly interesting that many of these characteristics are actually attributes in the knowledge-based economy. For example, it is often said that women are naturally too emotional for business decision making. In fact, emotion and more specifically "emotional intelligence" are highly desirable in the knowledge-based economy and assists in decision making particularly in aspects of human resources. According to Charles Handy, the management style of women fulfils the demands of new organisations better than their male counterparts. Women are better managers because of their qualities of adaptability, the ability to juggle several tasks at a time, are overall more interested in getting things done rather than seeking status or title, they are more instinctive and intuitive than men, tough but tender, focussed but friendly. Further criticism, particularly in the Middle East is that a woman's role as mother and housewife would be impossible if she were to take on an additional role outside the domestic arena. However, these judgements are being proved wrong by the growing number of role models for young women in the region who are proving that a balanced life is possible, together with growth in western-style day-care centres in addition to centralised family support.

Furthermore, there are many concerns that family members of women seeking employment have with regard to their female relatives entering the workplace. These are often cultural and religious concerns, for example that a woman would have to touch a man she barely knows, she would have to work nights and that she would have to have one-on-one meetings with men, all of which are cultural taboos.

It is important that these issues are approached in a sensitive yet appropriate way. It is perfectly in keeping with Arab and Islamic tradition for women and men to interact in matters of business provided it is done in a manner that respects these traditions. For example, in the West, it is considered totally normal for one man and one woman to conduct a business meeting in a closed office. In the Islamic world however, it would be construed as unseemly to conduct a business meeting in such a manner. Contrary to the implication, this does not mean that a meeting could not take place but rather that the meeting should include others where possible or that it is conducted in an open plan office or more public business environment.

The discovery of crude oil and its commercial production in the UAE created a new economic situation that was reflected in the availability of substantial financial resources on one hand, and the investment of such resources by the government for development on the other. The country has emerged into the mainstream of modernism over the past 40 years, with an economy driven by oil and gas and more recently by tourism. The population has been directly influenced by the rapid development witnessed by the country in recent years.

Over two thirds of university graduates in the UAE from government universities are Emirati women. However, women as a whole account for less than 12% of the entire workforce of the country. Furthermore, if the number of employees in the areas of Health and Education were removed, the figure would be substantially less. What is worse is that very few of those who make it to the labour market, make it to the boardrooms or upper echelons of leadership and management.

However immense societal changes do not come over night. It needs time for all people and for the system to adopt. What is important are the directions and support that the rulers of a country give. Such a direction and support for women in education and in the workforce is well established by those in power in the UAE. HH Sheikh Zayed bin Sultan Al-Nahyan, the former President of the UAE, said:

"The means to develop a country and modernise its infrastructures is a magnificent burden that should not be taken up by men only. The loss would be huge, for women

will be paralysed without any participation and productivity. It would lead to an unbalanced rhythm of life. Hence, women's participation in public life is required and we must be prepared for it."

And: *"Nothing could delight me more than to see woman taking up her distinctive position in society. Nothing should hinder her progress. Like men, women deserve the right to occupy high positions, according to their capabilities and qualifications."*

It may be concluded therefore that although women in Emirati society have come a very long way towards achieving equality, societal attitudes need to change towards their role if it is seen to be anything more than merely an increase the number of women in the workforce. Though Emirati society has therefore made great strides in this direction, it needs to go further in understanding that equal opportunity is more than a courtesy, but rather the right of all citizens.

ISLAMIC TRADITIONS

As in all Arabian Gulf countries, the constitution of the UAE is based on Islamic principles with the Sharia forming the basis of law and penal codes. The state religion of the UAE is thus Islam, though there is a growing presence of religious minorities due to economic migration into the country. Predominant amongst these are adherents to Christianity from Europe and the Far East and Hinduism from south Asia.

Gender inequality in the Middle East in general and in the Arabian Gulf region in particular, has socio-economic and political roots as opposed to religious roots. In order to understand this fully, an historical overview of Islam is needed. Such an analysis demonstrates that there is a wide gulf between Islam and cultural practices misconstrued as Islamic. It is thus important for women in the region to be familiar with Islam in its true sense rather than through cultural biases for emancipation and liberation to occur. Islam accords equal rights to both men and women. Yahya M., an American convert to Islam said:

"At the beginning, Islam was the most revolutionary liberalisation of women's rights the civilised world had ever seen. But afterwards Muslims became ignorant of this and now Muslim countries are the scene of some of the worst abuses of women's rights."

Visibly forced marriage, imposed polygamous marriage, female infanticide, honour killings and denial of basic education for girls are just some of the cultural practices wrongfully attributed to Islam. In contrast, Islam in its essence gives women the rights such as owning property and business, participation in choosing their leaders, participating in elections and standing for political office, freedom of speech, rights to education and inheritance and independent wealth. In UAE, in accordance with the rights and privileges laid down in the state religion, Islam, on which the Constitution is based, the right of women with regard to the inheritance of property are also guaranteed by law. The guarantees laid down for the rights of women in the UAE Constitution have been carried through effectively into other legislation passed since the establishment of the state. Sheikha Fatima stresses that the right of UAE women to effectively participate in the development of society is assured by the UAE constitution, which established equality between men and women in rights and duties. She says:

"This support for women stems from the teachings of the Islamic religion and the heritage and traditions of the UAE as well as the prudent view of President His Highness Sheikh Zayed bin Sultan Al Nahyan. It gives women the opportunity to reach the highest echelons of education, penetrate all fields of work, establish a foothold in society and asserts their belief in their own abilities and justify the faith of the society in them".

What has been noticeable in the UAE in recent years, is thus a shift away from those cultural practices which have restricted and stifled women from full participation in society, to an acknowledgement of a woman's worth based on Islamic principles. This has been supported by allowing political participation, the right to a full education including higher education, drives to eradicate female illiteracy, legal guarantees in employment, and improvements in health and welfare. Other initiatives that have benefited women in the UAE include the establishment of a marriage fund, which has had the effect of a reduction in the spinster population. Furthermore, there has been active promotion of these rights through various media. For example, international conferences, such as the Women as Global Leaders conference which is held by Zayed University and attended by women of international renown, are a reflection of the willingness of the rulers to move the nation positively toward change.

With these strides, problems still remain. Much remains to be done, partly because of constraints placed on female employment by social attitudes. Some UAE men, for example, are opposed to women working at all, while others will approve of female members of their family only working in areas of activity in which they do not come into contact with men. While women's participation in education exceeds that of men, their share in the workforce is still relatively weak and the traditions that hold them back remain strong. Women from wealthier families, who have a better chance for higher education, often fail to realise their full potential. Most educated women prefer jobs more suited to their social status rather than jobs consistent with their qualifications or ability. Despite all the incentives and official encouragement given to them to continue education, many young women and girls leave school early to marry and perhaps raise children. Then again notably, dowry issues for marriage, which are based on Islamic tradition and citizenship rights for non-Emirati husbands of Emirati women, are just two issues surrounding the welfare and development of UAE society which are intertwined with UAE women's issues. Affluence in UAE society has led to the expectation of large dowries and lavish wedding receptions, discouraging men from marrying. Many Emirati women therefore remain unmarried or seek foreign partners.

EXTENDED FAMILY NETWORKS AND CHILDCARE PROJECTS

The view that a woman's role as mother and housewife would be impossible to fulfil if she were to take on an additional role outside the domestic arena is being proved wrong by the growing number of energetic young women in the region who are proving that a balanced life is possible. Growth in western-style day-care centres in addition to centralised family support helps to live a balanced life. Family-friendly policies, such as flexible working hours and periods of leave, designed to help employees to balance work and family demands are of value. In this regard, the UAE is already ahead of the game. Centralised families allow for day care provision within the family unit. This, together with the ease of hiring domestic help in the UAE allows working mothers the growing freedom and flexibility to join the workforce. Most government institutions as well as some private UAE companies have also responded to the needs of their female employees by offering childcare services at the workplace. The Dubai Women Establishment, an initiative by a female member of Dubai's ruling family, is currently working on setting up model daycare centres. It is the specific aim of the National Corporate Child Care to enhance working opportunities as well as job satisfaction for hard-working mothers. Emirati staff will be employed in the nurseries.

Success Stories

The following part of the book includes profiles of Emirati women with various backgrounds and occupations. The information is based on personal interviews conducted between August 2007 and February 2008.

Fatima Obaid Khalifa Al Jaber

Fatima Obaid Khalifa Al Jaber is the Chief Operating Officer of Al Jaber Group, a large construction business founded by her father and based in Abu Dhabi. Beside her work in the family's business, Fatima Al Jaber is acting as a board member of Abu Dhabi Chamber of Commerce and Industry, the deputy chairman and member of the executive committee of the Abu Dhabi Businesswomen Council and a board member of The National Investor. In 2006 she was voted by Forbes Arabia as the 8th most influential woman in the Arab world.

Fatima Al Jaber was born in 1965 in Al Ain and finished her primary education there. During the seventies her family moved to Abu Dhabi where her father started his business in the booming construction sector. After finishing the secondary education in Abu Dhabi, Fatima Al Jaber's career plans were partly influenced by her family but in the end she says that she made her own decisions.

"The way I was raised by my family was that I can take a decision of what I really like, and I think by watching my father work in construction, listening, watching what was happening, I became really interested in engineering. Being the eldest one, my father did not like me studying abroad. Usually when you have a boy brother who went ahead of you, you can go with him. But usually when you are a girl and the first child … they were not favorable of me traveling abroad. So they told me to go to the engineering faculty at UAE University in Al Ain. They said: try it if you like it. If you do not, we promise to let you travel. And I started there at the faculty of architecture and moved back to Al Ain as a university student. After five years, I graduated in 1987 with a degree in architectural engineering."

In the last year of her studies, Fatima Al Jaber had a work placement in the Public Works Department in Abu Dhabi which is responsible for all the buildings and services for the government of Abu Dhabi. The department offered her to join them after graduation which she did.

"I had a choice: I could go and have a try. Plus my father at that time was not really interested in letting me work with him because it was a tough environment for me. There were no women working in contracting or construction at that time. He helped me a lot when I told him I would join the Public Works Department. He was my biggest supporter, and he is still. I think that without his understanding I would not be in my position today."

During the 80s and the 90s, Fatima Al Jaber gained much experience at the department as the Emirate evolved quickly and exciting projects came up on a constant basis. Beside her work experience she says that she developed her personality and learned how to climb up one career step after the other.

In 1995 Fatima Al Jaber got married and stopped working for one year.

"At that stage in your life, you just have other priorities. At that time even my husband and I thought that I would try it for one year, try to stay at home, think about whether I wanted to continue here or there. I stayed for about one year, trying to live my life, starting something. After one year I thought: This is not me. I cannot just stay like this. But then I got pregnant with my second daughter. So I faced it and I said let us keep it for another time. But I spent the year not only with raising the children but also studying process management which gave me much valuable input."

After this period of her life Fatima Al Jaber went back to work for the Public Works Department and was raised to Assistant Undersecretary, a highly regarded post within the organization.

"I stayed at that position for four years and I gained a lot of experience there. I learnt much – from every position you learn really much. I managed to also have the management skills. Being able to look at things in a wider view and being able also to communicate with people these are very important things. You have to make judgments and take decisions which other people rely on. So it is about being able to see a global picture of an issue."

After a post as Assistant Undersecretary at the Public Works Department and later at Abu Dhabi Municipality Fatima Al Jaber moved to her father's company and became Chief Operating Officer.

"My father said: Why do you not join us? I felt so proud when he asked me that question. I worked so long, and then I thought: this is the best time to go back to my family's business. I was not really part of it previously. So when my father asked me to join them, at a time when the group was going through a total restructure, I felt it was the best time to join. I was not really planning for it, but when it came, it came, because I really love my father and I appreciate what he has done. Also seeing around me, a lot of work is moving to the private sector. The trend was

moving from government to private – a lot of outsourcing, a lot of partnerships with the private sector. So it looked to me as the best move, the correct move."

Her own professional success draw Fatima Al Jaber's interest to the evolvement of other women of her country's workforce.

"Before my position as Assistant Undersecretary I was not really looking for other women, I was focusing on my work. But then when you go into these higher positions, you find that you have to communicate with others. People start to look at you and say oh, you are on this position, is there any other woman? So you just start looking around and see how this environment is working. Who else is there? You start going to conferences, meetings, forums, and then you meet these women. By the late 1990s, I had the understanding and the awareness that we have to communicate together as women. At this time the Abu Dhabi Chamber of Commerce and Industry told me that there is a strategy of really empowering businesswomen and they asked me to join. This is where the Businesswomen Council started. It was not really a council at that time, just a gathering and seeing what we could do. Similarly things developed in Dubai."

The role of the councils was defined mainly to create a forum for women. They should meet and discuss issues of business.

"Men have a lot of places to meet and to discuss and to discuss even the business opportunities. For us women, we cannot be exposed to men that much. We cannot go to working sessions. As a woman, it is not easy. Even if you try it, it is not easy. So we think that through these councils, women can really come together, talk about certain opportunities, talk about certain problems that they face in their business environment, explain to us maybe if there are opportunities that they want to offer and that through the council can be brought forward. Sometimes women come from all over the GCC. It is empowerment, empowerment for women themselves that they are really able to start their business. And we also created attention from the society that these women are able and we have to help them and we should really ease the difficulties and obstacles that are in front of them."

Even with so much support and encouragement for today's businesswomen in the UAE, challenges remained.

"Always there are challenges – I do not believe that there is really a very soft and comfortable life. That is a dream, and I think we would also be bored of getting a life like that without challenges. Challenges create determination in our life – for me. I enjoy working in environments like this because this is really when you can make things happen. Maybe because we are women we always challenge ourselves to be better. It is in our nature. Always women have to work harder than men in order to accomplish their goals. It is not because they are not able to do it, but it

is the entire environment around them is really challenging them to do so. So it is a natural part of being a woman to be determined to do things and to face these challenges."

Fatima Al Jaber has five small children who need much attention and care. Satisfying their needs and being a successful businesswoman at the same time is a task that can hardly be managed without a supportive family.

"It is not easy! You need a superwoman to do this. It is not really comfortable; sometimes you really have to be cruel to yourself and your child too. Sometimes you spend more time with the children, trying to manage your working hours. Sometimes you become stressed more and more. But this is life. You have your work, and this is part of your personality. You cannot really just leave it. Then you have your family, and this is also part of you. You want to have a good family. You cannot just let it go. You have to really juggle between these things. You cannot be perfect in all of them. You have your ups and downs. Sometimes you are the best mother, but you are the worst in your work and it seems that you cannot do these things. Sometimes you would be flying high in your work and you could not manage to attend your children's' celebration at school. And this is where husbands can help. I try to sometimes – I would not say use my husband, but... get him involved in this. Sometimes men do not like to get involved too much in the children's activities, but I try to do it. And if I was not there, he would attend. He has been a great help and a big support. Fortunately also with my family when I travel, my mother and my sisters take care of my children when I am not at home. We are fortunate with extended families here in the UAE."

The UAE society adopts to the rapid changes in the country and therewith also forms a very new, well educated youth. The new generation's daily lives are very different compared to the lives their ancestors had.

"Women are considered as important members of the society, same as the men. All doors are open. It might be an issue in a few families, but I think they are very few. Now also our way of life is different. Now, the younger generation, their fathers and their mothers are highly educated. So you can imagine that they will appreciate that their children are working. Education makes a difference. This is one of the blessings that we have here in our country. The late Sheikh Zayed really focused on education, pushing everybody to have a good education. That meant a lot to us. It changed a lot of the understandings that really shaped our life. And of course I want the same for my daughters. I have five children now, four daughters and one son. Thank God. They are in their elementary education. My eldest daughter is in the sixth grade, the youngest is still at the nursery. I am really looking to give them the best education. Money we can give them all the time, it is not an issue. But education is the real wealth that you can give your children. I

was lucky that I was not forced into any of the decisions that I made in my life. I am also not willing to let them be forced into anything."

AYSHA AL HAMILI

Aysha Al Hamili is the first female pilot in the UAE and one of the youngest female commercial pilots in the world. Moreover she graduated as one of the ten top students in her 2005 class from Zayed University with a Bachelor of Arts in International Studies and is currently working on two Master degrees – one in air transport management and one in air safety management.

Aysha Al Hamili's passion for flying began at a very young age. It was a childhood dream that turned into reality. She is 26 years old now and looks back on 10 years of flying experience.

"I always wanted to be a pilot, ever since I was a kid. I always thought about airplanes. I loved airplanes. Even when I traveled and the cockpit door opened, I always had to take a peak and to sit inside. It was very exciting and it used to make me really emotional. When I turned 14, I started to speak to my father seriously about it: In the future I want to be a pilot."

Aysha Al Hamili convinced her father that flying is not just a dream or a passion but rather a goal that she plans to pursuit. For her 16th birthday, he took her to Jordan to fly gliders as her birthday present.

"So we went to the gliders club at the Royal Jordanian Flight Academy. Then I saw the gliders and I recognized that they have no engines, I did not want to fly an airplane without an engine. I looked at the planes in the flying school beside the glider club. We went to the Royal Jordanian Air Academy and had an interview with the director. My father asked him if it is possible for me to join, and he told us: she has to wait until her 16th birthday to have the private pilot license. So I started flying as a student pilot for almost 3 months and on my 16th birthday I got my private pilot license."

After finishing her first license Aysha Al Hamili wanted more. She planned on becoming a commercial pilot after high school while her father wanted her to go to university to study for a bachelor's degree.

"I did a pact with my dad since he was against me flying. Not because of flying, but he wanted me to get a university degree. So I said: I am going to get my licenses and then go directly to university. So I stayed in Jordan for a year and a half and I got my commercial pilot license, my instrument rating, my certified flying instructor and my certified flying instrument instructor license. In Jordan I stayed

in a UAE dorm monitored by the Embassy and there were many safety and security measures there. My dad used to visit me a lot and I spent the weekends with my father and family. It felt like they were there with me. Mostly the girls in the dorm were studying medicine, so they spent most of their time studying. They did not have time to go out, and neither did I. I had never spoken English before, so when I started flying my English was so weak that I spent about 90% of the time just translating from English to Arabic. But sometimes the UAE girls and I would go as a group to have coffee."

Aysha Al Hamili studied hard and left school as a well trained pilot ready for entering employment. However this became the most difficult part of her career.

"After finishing all the necessary certificates, I came back to the UAE and I searched for a job. There were no female pilots back then in 2001. The men worried about my social/marital status and the fact that I was a women meant that on some point I might get married and have a family life and in their eyes I would not be able to fulfill the contract. Although I was not married or planning marriage, yet they were still thinking about it from these perspectives. I was not able to land the jobs I applied for because of those reasons. The first question they asked was: are you going to get married anytime soon, are you going to get pregnant anytime soon? I answered: no, I am 18 years old. I am not going to go anywhere. I am here. I am going to sign a ten years contract. But in the end it did not work."

So it was the right time for Aysha Al Hamili to fulfill the other part of the pact with her father. She went to study at university. She was successful but she started to miss flying. When her pilot licenses were about to expire it was impossible for her father to hold her back from flying. So beside her studies Aysha Al Hamili started to fly at a flying school again and that is when she found her first employment at Abu Dhabi Aviation, a domestic airline.

"I did an interview with the lower management and they said: Aysha, this is a job only for men. On the islands that we fly to there are no women whatsoever. There are no females. There are no bathrooms for females. It would be difficult and you would have to watch it. I told them just to give me the job and I will prove myself. So they ended up handing over my application papers to the chairman. They were actually pretty sure that I am not getting the job. But the chairman believed that I can do it, and told every one, give her a chance and let her prove herself, her performance will determine whether she will stay or not."

Aysha Al Hamili proved herself in theory and practice. After five years of flying experience in the company she was ready to become a flight captain, the highest position in a career as a pilot. When she fulfilled the minimum requirements to be a Captain on a Dash–8 airplane, it was unfortunate that she faced uncertainty about her development from the lower management again. Therefore she started to apply at other airlines and ended up with two offers: one as a commercial pilot in Sharjah, about 150 km away from her home, and one as an inspector at General Civil Aviation Authority in Abu Dhabi. It was a difficult decision for her but she finally took the offer in Abu Dhabi on condition that she will be allowed to work as inspector as well as an active pilot.

"It was very hard for me, because I live in Abu Dhabi and my family lives in Abu Dhabi. So if I took the job in Sharjah I would have had to relocate ... finally I decided to start to work with the General Civil Aviation Authority in Abu Dhabi. That was the best, most mature job I ever had. I like the responsibilities. It is like an octopus in aviation – you see every aspect in aviation. I used to see only flying and regulations and everything pertaining to flying. But now it is about how airplanes fly, and how you get the permissions, how planes and airports are certified, how every single person is certified and how the aviation industry is put together. It is just so fascinating! After about six months the director general said to me: Aysha, I see you in the air transport department. You have a political background and you are a pilot, this is really an advantage for you. Most of the people in our air transport department do not have the physical experience as a pilot or engineer or being in the field."

Aysha Al Hamili did not only revolutionize the airline industry in the UAE as the first female pilot and successful inspector. In fact she has already started to become a role model on an international basis when she delivered a speech at the International Civil Aviation Authority, a specialized agency under the United Nations responsible for air traffic rules and based in Montreal, Canada.

"They wanted me to prepare a few things on my life as well as some background details on the UAE and the women in the UAE for a meeting which was supposed to be for the empowerment of women in the industry. It was meant to be for about 30 people. However we ended up with almost 100 people listening, including highest ranking people of the organization. I was a bit nervous when I saw the entire crowd. I had my notebook with me and I had some figures about the number of women in the UAE who are educated, the number of women who are in high positions, the number of this, the number of that, facts, facts, facts. So I just looked at it. And I looked at them. I started the speech with a greeting, saying how honored I was. And then I said – since you are here, you do not want to hear about facts! You can search the internet and look for the facts! I started to just talk about the UAE to give them an idea of my country and I said: Men are going to start fighting for

rights soon! So you do not need to worry about the women's rights here, you need to worry about the men's rights. I went on to tell them about my experiences, and it was a great experience. They told me: you need to do it again!"

Surprisingly enough working in a hundred percent male environment created lesser problems for Aysha Al Hamili in reality than anyone would expect.

"From my first day on in a 100% male environment, no women whatsoever, I was wearing my pilot uniform and I was going to work and everything was so easy! People were respectful. I have never been harassed; I have never even been looked at. They got used to me so fast. It was very comfortable. When I started flying, I was the youngest pilot in the company. They were treating me like their youngest daughter or their sister and they were taking care of me. Until today there are a lot of people who think that flying is only for men. Even though I am there, but people say I am doing a man's job. No, it is not a man's job, get over yourselves! Nothing is just a man's job anymore. With technology you do not need muscles to fly an airplane, you need brains instead."

Beside her successful and passionate work Aysha Al Hamili has a number of hobbies. Especially sport fills up the small gaps in her daily calendar.

"I wake up around 5 am, usually get ready for figure skating. I do this twice a week. So I wake up, I warm up at home, do some pilates for 15 minutes, then I go to the ring from 5:45 to around 7. I take a quick shower and go to work. When I finish work, I usually go home and take a 40 minute nap. Before that, I sit with my dad for about two hours to give him a report about my day, because my dad is so interested in my life. I have a very good relationship with my dad. After the nap I sit with my family for a bit. We chat a little bit, and then we might go outside. But usually I try to stay at home from 7 pm onwards to do my research for the Master's degree. I do research and I read books. Sometimes I watch DVDs about flying for about two hours before I go to bed. On a very busy day I would go to bed at around 10 pm, maximum 11."

Being independent and having an exceptional career as a woman in a traditional Arab society does not mean being allowed to pass over certain rules. Good up brining and self-discipline are the basis for combining both aspects in Aysha Al Hamili's life.

"Freedom depends on the individual's definition of it, and this definition varies from one person to another depending on the background, environment and other factors that contribute to an individual's up-brining. To me, there are no restraints with regard to tradition. I am exercising my full freedom. Still for me, I am putting my own limits. My life is not about partying and going out and having a lot of

friends. I only have a few very good friends who are open-minded and whom I can have constructive arguments with. I can learn from them. Due to my job, I have to mix with men and I mainly deal with men. My job requires traveling and staying away from my family for weeks. I can do all this without any objection from my family, so the way I see it, my freedom is being fulfilled. My father is very open minded when it comes to studies or career development, to the extent that if I want to go to the moon to study something, he says go. My father trusts me so much and he believes that no mater where I am or what I do, and no matter how much he restrains me, if I want to make a mistake I will do it regardless of his supervision. For him what people think about his children is their perspective and their problem. I always try to be up to my father's expectations especially when it comes to freedom so I draw my own limits to the extent I see suitable both for myself and my family. Because of my family I am exercising my freedom, I think better than others."

One might also ask how this young and successful lady is handling her own family life in future. Aysha Al Hamili's view on that is very open-minded.

"It seems that women who are strong and independent find it more difficult to find the right guy. I believe in that strongly. I think that if I ever get married, it has to be somebody who is strong and confident enough to be able to cope. I would compromise my career as long as it does not jeopardize my development, but no matter what criteria I put for my future husband I believe that I cannot control this matter, it is fate that controls it."

So the most interesting question remains open: Where will we see Aysha Al Hamili be in 10 years from now?

"The initial plan was to get my flying hours and be a captain before I reach the age of 30. Now, I am on another course and I have to balance between my office job and flying. Whether that can lead to a very high position we will see … the UAE vision is for women to go high. And I believe that with my qualifications I can reach high in the aviation field. I feel that I am very qualified for my age and I need just time to gain more experience. So I am going to give myself time and enjoy what I am doing. I can see myself reaching high if I continue on that path. You never know, anything can happen and just change the course. But as long as I am alive, I will continue learning. I believe that there is no limit to how much one can learn or how far they can reach if they believe in themselves."

At the end of the interview with Aysha Al Hamili her father joined and told us about his enjoyment but also anxiety during his daughter's career in a cockpit. However it is obvious how proud he is of her and her achievements:

"Many foreigners do not know much about our culture, good or bad. They do not know about our education ... My ancestors came from the desert, but we are not closed minded, and we are not closed to the world, because of them we are where we are today. I support all my children when it comes to education. I believe that my daughter is gifted, sometimes God gives something to somebody that others do not have. I am not just saying that because of my daughter – I am proud of all the women who created something new and something that contributed to the development of this country. Those women are the roles models and they are the ones who pave the way for others to follow."

Aysha Al Hamili's life might be an on going dream, but it was realistic steps that she took with the support of her family that materialized her childhood dreams.

DR. HOURIYA KAZIM

Dr. Houriya Kazim is the UAE's first female surgeon. She specializes in breast surgery and has recently opened her own clinic, the Wellwoman Clinic. Dr. Houriya Kazim is very active in spreading awareness about breast cancer. Her Breast Cancer Research Foundation works with cancer survivors and researches genetic causes to breast cancer. Money for this foundation is raised through donations and special activities such as walkathons or dragon boat racing – Dr. Houriya and the Tickled Pink Paddlers, a group of cancer survivors, raced to second place in Penang in 2007.

Dr. Houriya Kazim's profession seems to be her family's calling – about 60 to 80 of her relatives work in medicine or related fields. It all started with her grandfather who was a Hakim, a faith healer who helped people through prayer and meditation.

"My father tells me that once a year or so, his father would lock himself into a room for days with just water and the Koran. His kids would be listening at the door, wondering what is happened to Baba. And Baba was chanting away from the Koran. I think there is actually a lot to be said about that – in modern life, our brain is so full of so many things that we do not actually develop those powers that perhaps we have to heal others or to heal ourselves. That was certainly his thing."

Even though Dr. Houriya Kazim's grandparents were not formally educated, her grandmother had the foresight to send her children to India, which was a British colony at the time – all seventeen of them. This was in the 1940s, at a time when the UAE was yet to be founded and higher education was not yet available. Dr. Houriya Kazim's grandfather owned a Dhow, the traditional boat of Gulf merchants. This Dhow was used as transportation, and because there were no hotels at that time, merchants used to own houses in their major port of calls. With transportation and accommodation covered, the students still had to cover their school fees. Dr. Houriya Kazim's father made his way through his medical school by winning the award as best student every year which won him a scholarship for the following year. His brothers and sisters also went to medical school in India, and the elder ones usually helped out the younger ones financially. When they graduated in the 1950s, there was no point in coming back to the UAE as there were no hospitals at that time. After working in Trinidad for a while alongside his brother who had met and married an Indian woman, a descendent from the indentured laborers in the Caribbean, Dr. Houriya Kazim's father got married to a woman from Dubai and then moved to England, taking with him his daughter Houriya who was three months old at the time. In the early 1960s, the family moved back to Trinidad where Dr. Houriya Kazim attended primary school. Even though the society in Trinidad was quite liberal, her parents were strict, and in their house, the children were brought up as if they were in Dubai.

When her best friend decided to attend boarding school in Canada, Dr. Houriya Kazim wanted to go as well. At first her parents did not approve.

"My parents were horrified because my parents are the type – anytime anybody moved, everybody moved like a clan. If I went to a birthday party, all the people in my family would have to go to the birthday party as well. It is a tribal thing, I guess, the whole tribe has to go. So when I announced that I wanted to go to boarding school, everybody looked at me like I had gone mad."

A lot of insisting as well as a trip to Canada to evaluate the school which turned out to be an all girls school out in the woods with no man under 65 anywhere in sight finally brought the parents' permission. The boarding school was a Christian school, as had been the primary school in Trinidad.

"We got a very good education in the Christian schools. Obviously there were some Christian activities of which your parents could exempt you. But my parents never did because they did not want us to be fooling around for an hour every week. They figured it was safer for us to be in the class learning about Jesus than being out roaming the playground! My parents really brought us up in a very healthy way of looking at Islam. I never considered converting to Christianity because I did not see the need to give up a religion I was happy with. I did not find anything in my religion that really bothered me. It is an extremely tolerant religion and I think it is really very modern in its outlook. So I never converted, even though all my schooling has been Christian schooling."

There was never any doubt that Dr. Houriya Kazim was not going to go to university. In her family, it was more or less expected, even though no one pressured her to do medicine. Even though all her father's brothers and sisters had university degrees, a lot of their cousins never got any formal education. Their daughters in turn were never encouraged to attend school.

"I do have family where the girls are not pushed. But I always thought it was their choice to not have a career. I never really thought that I had a choice because I know my parents so well! They would never have gone for that! But I never really stopped to think that I could have done something else. "

The decision to study medicine was probably influenced by her environment, or it may have been in her blood. Dr. Houriya Kazim went to medical school in Ireland. She came back to Dubai in 1988 and worked for Rashid Hospital for two years as an intern in general surgery. Her male colleagues were very supportive. Since most of the women preferred being examined by a female doctor, there was an obvious need for female surgeons and the group helped each other out where they could.

"I did not feel any competition. We were all fighting the same things – coming as outsiders and working your way into the system. Also, the work is very hard physically. You could not pay me to do that again!! There is no amount of money that you could give me to do that again. We were all exhausted and tired and had to study and do exams. There was a certain comradely with sufferers like you."

When it came time to do a post graduate degree, Dr. Houriya Kazim went to the UK and sent an application for a temporary position to a famous cancer center, the Royal Marsden Hospital. She attached a small note to her CV that said "I really want this job. And when the six months are over I am gone. I will leave you and you can hire whomever you want". Dr. Kazim got invited to an interview and was the first one out of a large number of applicants to be called back in – something that she had not expected and was so surprised at that when she was tossed a list of open position, she randomly picked the first one on the list – breast. On her way back home she realized that she would now have to be working with female patients only – the thought was depressing. But on her first day at work, she realized she had found her calling and has not regretted doing this specialty since even though it can be emotionally draining.

"My surgical colleagues treat me like I am in kindergarten most of the time. They are doing big surgeries, whipping out spleens and stomachs and colons, and they think that breast surgery is actually kindergarten. Surgically, it may not be that

technical. But as a whole – I tell people I am more of a psychiatrist than a surgeon because most of my patients think they have breast cancer and of course most of them do not have it. So it is really about trying to assess them and then convince them that they are fine and that they are going to be fine. It is draining mentally rather than physically."

After working as a breast surgeon in London until 1997, Dr. Houriya Kazim went back to Trinidad for a few months to work for free. In early 1998, she did a fellowship in Houston, Texas for a few months where she also got married to her long-time fiancé whom she had met in Dubai through friends. The American journalist who covered wars had waited nine years for his fiancée to finish the long and hard road to becoming a specialized surgeon. Even though Dr. Houriya Kazim has no regrets, she does not want to encourage her children to go into medicine.

"It is a lot of time and a lot of suffering. 90 to 100 hours per week were considered normal. I have literally slept with mops and brooms in the cupboard because it was the only dark place I could find. I tell people that if they really love their children, they would not want that for them. There were times when the beep went off and I burst into tears because I could not physically move. It is much pressure. And then when you go home you have to study for your exams after all of that! You cannot pay me to do that again, as much as I love what I am doing now!"

Dr. Houriya Kazim came back to Dubai in 1998 and has been working here ever since. She first started out at Welcare Hospital and then moved to Emirates Hospital. It was during this time that she had her two daughters. Balancing work and the family was quite a challenge as flexible working hours were still a novelty and relying on an extended family network was not an option in a family were most of the women had their own work. Her parents lend a helping hand when they could, and Dr. Houriya Kazim manages by employing two nannies, one of whom she calls her domestic manager. It is important for her to devote herself to her children as much as to her work.

"Once I get to work I try not to deal with anything at home unless it is an emergency or the school is calling. I do not deal with home when I am at work. When I go home it is the same thing. I do not answer my phone unless it is coming from a hospital and it is one of my patients or something else that is urgent. Otherwise my time is just for my kids because I do not have that much time with them."

Working in the UAE, Dr. Houriya Kazim has come across a lot of very advanced cases of cancer and realized the need to spread awareness about the prevention and cure of this disease. She started out by going to universities as well as the hinterland to give lectures about self-examination. The hospital also organized an information booth in a shopping mall and they encouraged people to do appointments. From there, patients started donating small sums of money to do further awareness projects, which was the beginning of Dr. Houriya Kazim's Research Foundation. They are currently working on a goodie bag for breast cancer surgery patients which will be distributed to all private and government hospitals free of charge. The bag was designed by herself. It includes items such as pillows to protect the breast (made by the Dubai Quilter's Guild) as well as pouches for drain bags and notepads and pens to put down information the doctor gives – things that cancer survivors have told in research that they would have liked to have. The Foundation is also working on videos and DVDs in different languages with information about breast cancer.

Dr. Houriya Kazim also tries to help women who have decided to go into surgery. It still is not easy. Even though the numbers have improved a lot since Dr. Houriya Kazim's time in the UK (women made up only 2% of surgeons at the time), it is still very much a male-dominated field and women are at the bottom of a hierarchy that is determined by gender as well as ethnicity. Female surgeons are submitted to a lot of pressure, not the least of which coming from the families. In general, Dr. Houriya Kazim finds that even though a lot of women are now working, only very few of them actually stay the course and make it to the top.

"There is no discrimination for women or men and the government certainly encourages young people as a whole to go into business. Most of the women are formally educated. You have access to getting on that ladder. But what I want to know is why those women are getting off the ladder. Why are they not staying the course? Why do we not have more women in very high places? I think a lot of it has to do with the pressure from the family and the husband. I still see quite a lot of that and I find it quite surprising. Do I think that it may be overcome? It is probably a generation thing. People change and certainly the way Dubai is going economically, families are now going to need a double income. Men still find it hard to accept that though, especially if their mothers were stay-at-home moms. If you come from a family where your mother worked, then it is a different thing and you will understand it. Now if women have to go to work, her sons are not going to think of it as such an alien idea."

Many UAE nationals feel that their traditional values are threatened by working women as well as the new ways of life brought in by all the international expatriates. To Dr. Houriya Kazim, the key lies in child-rearing. In her childhood abroad, there were all kinds of influences – different religions, different races, even different eating habits. But she always went back to what her parents taught her. She also insists that Dubai has always been a melting pot.

"So the fact that we all speak so many languages or that we all look a little different and dress a little different – it has always been like that in Dubai. When I look at old pictures of my grandfather I see him with his head tied with a koffiya (the black-and-white headpiece) but I also see him in a suit. It was a normal thing to do when you interacted with different people – and there were always different people here! That is our culture! Being brought up the way I was with all the different kinds of people in my life is not a bad thing because it actually made me a better and more tolerant person. It makes me more acceptable of people and religion. I teach my children the same. They go to a British school but they do Islamic studies and they know that we are Muslims. There is an international student body at the school so they learn about everything. We put out the clay pots for Diwali on our door steps, the diyas and I explain to them what it is about and why we do it. And at Christmas we do the Christmas thing and for Eid we definitely do the Eid thing. I know there are people here who probably would have a problem with it but I do not. I think you have to see how the world is going. We cannot go into these little caves now. It is a world of globalization. It does not mean you will lose your religion or your culture. It just means that you can be what you are and then you accept everything else around you."

DR. MESHGAN AL AWAR

Dr. Meshgan Al Awar is currently the Director of the Research and Studies Center at Dubai Police Academy. She also serves as a member of the Higher Committee and Secretary General of the prestigious Zayed International Prize for the Environment, and as Managing Editor of the Society & Environment Magazine.

Dr. Meshgan Al Awar has represented the UAE abroad and serves as regional expert on many programs for the United Nations. In 2005, she was appointed coordinator of the Arab region for the United Nations Non-Governmental Organizations Informal Regional Network, she is the UAE representative in the Arab Network for Women in Science and Technology (UNESCO) and was nominated as an expert and prospective member of a Regional Scenario Team for one of the UN Environment Program's seven global sub-regions to support the development of the 4th Global Environment Outlook (GEO-4) in the First Global & Regional Scenarios Development Meeting of GEO-4 in Bangkok in 2005.

As an expert in her field, she has been invited several times as guest speaker at the American FBI Academy, and she is a visiting faculty to the Center for Remote Sensing at the Boston University. She has recently been invited to lead the United Nation's Center of Excellence for the Education of Sustainable Development in the Arab region through the Non-Governmental Organizations Informal Regional Network (UN-NGO-IRENE). Not even the sky is the limit to Dr. Meshgan Al Awar: she was offered a participation certificate by Office of Space Science (NASA) in Mars Exploration Rover Mission 2003.

Born and raised in Dubai as the eldest daughter of five children, Dr. Meshgan Al Awar says she owes everything to her mother:

"My inspiration in life was my mother. She encouraged me at every step through school and college. She was an extraordinary lady whose physical confinement to her kitchen and home did not limit her from dreaming an ambitious future for her children. She wanted us to set out and create something out-of-the-ordinary."

All the Al Awar siblings are big achievers today, occupying prominent positions in public and professional life. As the eldest, Dr Meshgan Al Awar gave the lead early in life when she did her bachelor's degree in chemistry and geology at the UAE University in Al Ain. She then started her professional career as a teacher in chemistry, the first Emirati female to do so.

"After I got my bachelor's degree, I was very keen to give back the knowledge that I gained in chemistry to high school students. However it was a challenge because I was the first UAE national to teach chemistry at high school level. People used to think that foreigners were better teachers than us. So I had to prove myself and I did it. And it was fun. It teaches you about leadership, because you have to lead the class: the presentations, the skills of leadership, and to deal with people with different characteristics. I believe teachers have another important role to play in nation-building: They need to present the material in an attractive way so that students get interested retain the knowledge. I established the first chemistry club, in which I managed to organize many activities and projects. Students greatly benefited from this because they had to apply the knowledge they gained in classrooms and create something new."

At the age of 26, Dr. Meshgan Al Awar went to the University of Wales in Cardiff, UK, for her PhD. She went abroad together with her two young children and her husband who did his PhD in the field of media and mass communication. The family made a point of mixing with British families to enrich their experience of life in Britain and to get a real feel for the new culture. Dr. Meshgan Al Awar worked very hard on her PhD on "Reaction of Polyene sequences in poly (vinyl chloride)", sometimes spending 14 hours or more at the laboratory. Safety was always put first – a notion that

Dr. Meshgan Al Awar would take with her to Dubai later. She soon earned a very good reputation, publishing her results in international publications even before getting her PhD.

"I enjoyed taking on challenges at the university, and I still enjoy them now. It is the only way to prove your real worth to yourself and to society at large. Whenever there were obstacles I worked on solving them. When I submitted my thesis, I got it back with no corrections! After the PhD, the next major step for me was to apply the knowledge in my country."

Back home, Dr. Meshgan Al Awar returned to her beloved teaching profession and helped to update the existing chemistry curriculum at the time. However, she was also beginning to miss the excitement and pioneering spirit of scientific research and development. So when she was offered the position of a chemistry expert in the general department of forensic sciences at Dubai Police she took her chance. Over the years she not only helped in solving the daily challenges but also managed to bring about great changes to the department.

"While I was working in the forensic science department, I developed a manual for safety precautions and a safety code of practice for laboratories," she reminisces.

Dr. Meshgan Al Awar's natural ability to innovate and accomplish major improvements in her work soon became an open secret to her superiors and the leaders of the country. In 1999, she was honoured as the best female employee under the Dubai Government Excellence Program. It was time to use this potential for the development of the country in general and for its international reputation in particular.

"I was appointed as a member of the higher committee of Zayed International Prize for the Environment by HH Sheikh Mohammed Bin Rashid Al Maktoum in 1999. Since that time, I tried to implement the patron's vision in every step we took. Today, this prize has established itself as one of the most prestigious environmental prize worldwide. I have also taken part in promoting the prize at home and abroad through United Nations programs, press conferences in Europe, at the World Summit on Sustainable Development in Johannesburg and wherever possible. Through my experience I have come to realize that it's not policy but implementation that is the real challenge most societies face. Nation-building is about much more than giving a lecture or talking about sustainability. The way we do this is by constant research and the right approach to the development of different segments of the society."

The Zayed International Prize for the Environment now enjoys consultative status with the UN Economic and Social Council, and Dr. Meshgan Al Awar has devoted a lot of time and energy on her work with the UN Environment Program. It may have been this involvement on an international level that prompted her to be nominated as one of the first female candidates in the first ever election to the Federal National Council of the UAE.

She ran her campaign under the slogan "What is difficult we do today, what is impossible we do tomorrow." During her campaign, which was acknowledged as one of the most informed and professionally run, she stressed an approach of "open hearts and open minds" to encourage cultural understanding between UAE nationals and the expatriate community in the country. Dr. Meshgan Al Awar ran a tough race and came within a few votes of being elected, but many of her ideas are now being implemented.

Being a woman was never an issue for Dr. Meshgan Al Awar in her long career, even in a conservative society like hers. For her, ambition doesn't stop with the achievement of a goal.

"Our leaders support the role of women. Women are everywhere now. I would even say that today men will have to fight for their rights in this new world. But what matters most is not the numbers but the results." Dr. Meshgan Al Awar believes that *"it is neither the gender nor the degree that make a leader. Leadership starts with a vision and grows on a combination of knowledge, experience, and attitude."*

While Dr. Meshgan Al Awar builds her reputation internationally, she always finds enough time for her family in her schedule. She is personally very involved in her children's education and well-being.

"I believe that being different is not an act of rebellion, but rather an inspiration for change. It is also the need of the day in this 21st Century. Today, women must be better prepared to take care of themselves than in their mothers' generation."

The UAE has set new records in education since its formation in 1971. There are more Emirati females outnumber males graduating out of colleges. Highly educated, socially aware and resolute, Dr. Meshgan Al Awar has devoted more than a quarter of a century to the betterment of education, science, environment, civil administration and public service. Therewith she is a role model for the emerging generation of women in the UAE.

HABIBA AL MARASHI

Habiba Al Marashi is the Chairperson and Co-founder of the Emirates Environmental Group based in Dubai. The Emirates Environmental Group is a voluntary, non-government organization devoted to protecting the environment through the means of education, action programs and community involvement. The organization started in 1991 as a pioneer in its sector and now has more 1200 names on its mailing list, including individual and corporate members, federal and local government agencies, universities, colleges and schools as well as reputed international institutions.

Habiba Al Marashi is married and has four children. She comes from a family of professionals with siblings of both genders well established in their professions. Her late father believed in equity of education and opportunities for all his children and encouraged them to choose to work. So she was educated in the UAE, received a Diploma in Business Administration in the UK and started to work from a young age. Before co-founding the Emirates Environmental Group together with 11 other individuals, she worked for the Federal Chamber of Commerce & Industry and owned a florist business. Her hard work and dedication was acknowledged while working for the Dubai Development Board where she successfully out of her own initiative set up a dedicated department and team working towards the cause of the Environment – a one of its kind where perhaps the emphasis on Environmental issues was non-existent.

Habiba Al Marashi's work is her passion. While following her path she was and still is greatly inspired by the vision and policies of the first President of the UAE, the late His Highness Sheikh Zayed Bin Sultan Al Nahyan, who paved the way for environmentalism in the country and made it easier for campaigners like her to promote the environment among the community and other key sectors.

"I was initiated very early to the concept of environmental stewardship as my religion, Islam, taught me about it. I had an in-grained affinity for nature and creations of the natural world since my childhood ... My work on the environment is something that is a part and parcel of my thoughts, my feelings and indeed my being"

While being involved in a constant struggle between the daily management of the affairs of the Emirates Environmental Group as the Chairperson and giving the best shot towards social and family commitments Habiba Al Marashi remains sensitive and involved in the needs and requirements of her family and the society. She believes in giving quality time to her family but does not deny that it is sometimes exhausting to balance work and family and it leaves very little time for the individual himself or herself. While this is the price to pay, Habiba Al Marashi did not experience any moment of doubt about her professional involvement no matter how tough the journey has been or continues to be. She values management skills, professional competence and being a role model as key issues for both men and women in leadership. The combination of education and talent creates successful leaders. While education is vital for clarity in thought and purpose and sharpens both, some form of inherent quality to lead is also a vital factor – not all highly educated people are leaders, and not all leaders are uncut diamonds.

"I am a perfectionist in my professional work and I believe in leading by example. I have strived for constant improvement while setting my goals on performance and deliverables. I have always defined my values as well as my work in terms of my faith, culture, traditions, while simultaneously retaining a wider and global outlook."

Habiba Al Marashi faces two major challenges in her work. On the one hand, running an NGO means dealing with limited resources. On the other hand, influencing the mind sets of people of various nationalities who live in the UAE and cultivating a sense of stake in the environment means achieving a uniform commitment from various sectors, business and communities. While very often environmental commitment tends to rest in individuals rather than in communities or business cultures, it is challenging to keep the environmental drivers going on a continuous and long term basis.

As far as challenges for women in business are concerned, Habiba Al Marashi sees the differences between Emirati and Western business women – especially in Dubai – more and more diminishing. While there are no differences in business codes and practices compared to Western countries, businesswomen in the Gulf region still face stiffer challenges due to the social fabric. However, the working climate is transforming and can be expected to be a level playing field for all in the future.

Habiba Al Marashi leads the Emirates Environmental Group to achieve its goals and objectives on sustainable development, and to become the focal point across sectors to direct environmentalism in the country. For the women in her country she wishes more of them to become active and responsible contributors to the overall development of society, economic progress and environmental responsibility.

MARIAM BEHNAM

Mariam Behnam is a very active and sharp-minded 87-year old former diplomat in the service of the Iranian Education Ministry. Self-confidence, strength of mind and eloquence of speech are the outstanding traits of the lady who prides herself in being a "feminine feminist" and whose life tells the story of a remarkable struggle for independence.

Mariam Behnam was born in Southern Iran (Gulf region) in 1921 into a family of aristocrats, scholars and pearl-traders. Her family was very traditional and so it was the women whose word was law in child-rearing. Mariam Behnam's great-grandmother Monkhali in particular was a strong character set in her traditional ways who nonetheless seems to have been at a loss as to how to deal best with her great-granddaughter who was a very active child nicknamed "Zelzelah", Persian for earthquake, not only to reflect a natural disaster which occurred in the year of her birth. At the time of Mariam's childhood, individualism and independence were not conceivable for women. Her autobiography "Zelzelah – A woman before her time", recalls how Monkhali felt compelled to call the doctor to figure out what was wrong with her unusual great-granddaughter:

"He examined me thoroughly, all the time asking questions which I was uninhibited in answering. Finally he made his diagnosis: I remember the words to this day: The only thing wrong with this child is that she was born a few decades before her time. Monkhali's diagnosis was that the man had clearly taken leave of his senses and she pronounced his opinion worthless."

Mariam Behnam's childhood days were spent learning the Quran and Persian literature as well as traditional handicrafts. As the first girl in her family, she managed to trick her way into going to a public school. This allowed her to flee the stifling atmosphere of a superstitious household – one where for some time she was regarded as "manhoos" meaning "someone with a bad omen", and her supposedly cursed state was blamed for being responsible for the death of her younger brother. It is one of Mariam's most painful memories when the women decided to hold a burning stick to her neck to "drive out the evil". Strangely enough, the children born after her lived and soon her position changed later on as "khosh qadam" meaning "good omen". Instead of concentrating on her resentment though, she believes it will not do her any good to dwell on the negative aspects of her childhood or feel sorry for herself.

Mariam Behnam attended high school in Karachi where her family moved to from Bandar Lingah (Iran). After a short and mismatched marriage, she gave birth to her first-born son Essa in 1944. Returning to her family, she took up studies at the Punjab University of Lahore, becoming the first woman in her family to acquire a university degree. Taking up a career was met with many objections, but she nevertheless went to work as a teacher and later on took a job in the governmental sector in Teheran. In the 1950s, Mariam Behnam got married to Abdullah Pakravan, a widower with two children, Marie and Rokna. Two more daughters were soon to arrive, Shahnaz and Shirin. Not one to get settled with household routines, she set up a high school for girls in Bandar Abbas (Iran) and joined the Education Ministry, quickly rising through the rank to become Cultural Counsellor for the Ministry of Arts and Education in Lahore, later returning to Iran to become Director General of Arts and Culture in the Baluchistan and Sistan province.

Whereas her husband was a calm, gentle person who encouraged her work, it was still an unusual feeling for the men in her life to be affiliated with Mariam Behnam where usually women were recognized by their relationship with men.

"We used to go to parties, and people were asking about my husband – who is that gentleman? He is the husband of Mariam Behnam. I did not mind it, I liked it. Sorry, I liked it. The same thing happened to my father. He went to do something very special. They told him: Sorry, not this year, come back next year. What did you say was your name? He said: Abdulwahid Behnam. Are you related to Mariam Behnam? I am her father. Ooohhh … please sit down! So they spoke with each other and they finalized everything for him. He came home absolutely furious but he was just pretending though: What kind of a life is this! I go in person to a certain office; nobody takes notice of me, and my mission. In my position to go personally to an officer is unheard of. No sooner my relationship with you was established that everything changed in my favour! I answered: All my life I was your daughter. Today for one day, you are my father. Is something wrong with that?"

Mariam Behnam's professional life was spent implementing new projects, meeting high-ranking politicians and organizing conferences and seminars. It was a time filled with acknowledgment for her hard work, especially from the ruling leaders. During the political tensions in the late 1970s, Mariam Behnam feared that her position with the government would make her a target. She was nearing retirement age and so she decided it would be best for her to leave the country. She left Iran hardly ten days before it would have been impossible. Her name was soon on a blacklist of members of the old regime.

Immigrating to Dubai was a natural choice. Mariam Behnam had been coming to the emirate for decades as the majority of her family members settled here.

"Dubai was always a business hub, a very friendly place. Everyone who came here felt very much at home. They were very welcomed with open arms. So people just rushed and came here, and so did we, almost 150 years back. As a child, I used to hear two names, one was Dubai, one was Lingah. So for me to come to Dubai was easy – this is where my sister was married and the rest of the family stayed. I belonged to many families whose origins are from there, but of course now they are UAE nationals, they have proved how much they are a part of Dubai. They were there throughout the building and throughout what is happening now also. So it was so natural for me to get up, leave everything and come to Dubai. It was very much like home from Bandar Abbas and Bandar Lingah where I came from. And at the same time, it was the best of both the worlds. To me, it was an inspirational place. I felt that Dubai inspired us to get the best out of life. Which it did! For instance I wrote all my books here. Everything that I created, I created it here, or continuation of whatever I had done before."

Mariam Behnam had first come to Dubai in the late 1930s when it was still a very small place with a conservative society – no electricity, no running water, no paved roads, and hardly any freedom for the women who spent most of their time in their houses. To pass their time, Mariam entertained women who came to visit by religious chants or telling stories, and even to this day people remember her. Dubai was also the place of a brief career as a fortune teller which soon attracted people from as far away as Ajman who came by boat and Abra to enjoy Mariam's palm reading, which she confesses was mostly for show. But then maybe one of three "silly things" she said actually came true, so her reputation grew. Mariam felt active and fulfilled. She never hurt their feelings and shamed them. She gave hope and encouraged women to believe in themselves.

"What I have always done is to be with people, to attract people, to command people. Wherever I go, I cannot sit anywhere except it has to be at the top where I sit, overlooking everything. It has always been a position of leadership, position of authority, position of power, position of respect. Maybe all that I did had to do with the fact that though I was deprived of much attention, in the early days of my life the aristocratic attitude of our family women and constant reminding of being told to behave lady-like and dignified had something to do with it."

Soon she worked for the newly-established English newspaper Gulf News in Dubai. She wrote feature articles on Arab music, culture and society. Because her family had long-lasting ties with the area, she was granted UAE citizenship. Mariam Behnam's youngest daughter Shirin got married soon but Mariam Behnam did not stay without a daughter in her house for long as she soon adopted a five-year old orphan named Noora. Furthermore Mariam Behnam became active in the oldest founded "UAE Women's Society" run by her active sister Bibiya who had dedicated her time entirely to the community services of Dubai. Mariam was closely involved with the "Petroleum Wives' Club" which is now known as the "Dubai International Women's Club". Previously holding the post of president, she is now senior advisor to the Club. She describes it as her mission in life to bring people together. These responsibilities as well as her numerous friends ensure that Mariam Behnam never feels alone or old. In fact, her daughter Shirin says about her that she often forgets her age:

"Some weeks ago she said: I do not want to go to this event. I said: Why? She said: There are all old men and women there. I said: How old? She said: I do not know, really old. 70 years old. And it was totally innocent and I looked at her: I guess you are joking? She replied: No, they are really old, maybe about 70. And Mariam adds: Age is a matter of the mind, if they are and feel young and active, I do not mind!"

Whereas some might lament the changes that come with old age, Mariam Behnam is not one to focus on negative thoughts.

"I have no patience for negativity. There is so much positive energy in the world where you can be vibrant, when you can be lively, all the music in the air, all the rhythm in the air. You leave all that and sit down and lament – on what? I would rather thank God for my blessings and enjoy what I have."

Sitting down never became a favourite pastime of Mariam Behnam. She recently went to Pakistan for a world championship in her hobby Bridge. In fact, Mariam dreams of establishing a bridge federation in the UAE some day soon.

Mariam Behnam's daughters are now well-known figures. Her eldest Shahnaz enjoys a worldwide reputation in the media, having worked as presenter for the BBC and Al Jazeera and of course her contribution to Dubai where she has her roots and which is home to her and her family. Her youngest Shirin is now owner and co-founder of several businesses in Dubai. Shirin's daughters are in their twenties and all have a career. Mariam

Behnam is proud of the fact that when her grand-daughters will one day have children of their own, she will have lived to see seven generations. Looking back, she sees a huge difference between the younger generation's life and her own. She got everything fighting for it, and the constant obstacles were what pushed her on. This spirit is greatly admired by the younger females in her family:

"A lot of the nieces always say: I must be having auntie Mariam's blood. I suppose it is enough to have one figure in the family for other's to say: "Do not scold me, I am just following her." Somebody in front of me once asked a child: what would you want to become when you grow up? I want to be like auntie Mariam."

It is important for Mariam Behnam to see women reaching out for independence and fighting their way to the front:

"It is a source of delight and pride to see girls of the Gulf and the UAE in particular to reach heights and be achievers. The development of a nation is always measured by the active social participation of women. The UAE in a very short time has surpassed all human expectations in every field which needs volumes to describe in full. I do not believe in any woman being weak, I am sorry, any woman! Hands up for them. No woman, no woman. There are some people who do not know better, who have never seen better. You cannot expect anything from them. But those who know – I would always expect them to go ahead and fight for their rights if they cannot get there straight away."

SHIRIN ABDULRAZAK

Shirin Abdulrazak is the director of "The Living Zone" – two large franchised furniture and home ware stores called "Bombay" and "Zone". Furthermore she is the founder and director of the boutique "Candella" and "Sisters Beauty Lounge". All her businesses are based in Dubai.

Shirin Abdulrazak is the daughter of Mariam Behnam.

Between being born in the Bastak area in Iran and settling in Dubai, Shirin Abdulrazak lived in several countries around the world and she was educated in Iran, Pakistan, Switzerland, the UK and France. She was surrounded by two strong characters during her childhood – her mother Mariam Behnam who is a former diplomat and her older sister Shahnaz Pakravan, who is a television presenter formerly at Channel 33, BBC and Al Jazeera.

"I have lived under the shadow of strong women all my life … It has been quite a journey with them, and a great challenge. I remember when we were children people would ask me how old I am and my sister Shahnaz would answer: She is

nine. What do you do, little one, they would ask. And again the elder sister would say: She goes to school. I could not get a word in edgeways with this sister! When I was older and we were finally separated, that is when I tried to do my own thing, like speak for myself."

At around the age of 22, Shirin met and married Majid Abdulrazak, a prominent business man whose ancestors also hailed from Bastak and had settled in Dubai more than 100 years ago. Together they raised three daughters. Today these American educated daughters have entered the Dubai workforce. The eldest Rasha works with her mother in running the family businesses.

Shirin Abdulrazak started her own business at the age of 26 and from then on she has been an entrepreneur all her life. She founded and managed a manufacturing unit of an import-export business of school uniforms and professional wear, and five years ago she diversified into the present family run retail businesses.

"I had three little children in school in the early 80's, and everyone used to ask me about their beautiful school uniforms. And then one day I remember the head mistress of their school asking me if I would help in designing children's uniforms. The rest is history on that one. It amazes me that new business ideas always came to me through my children. A few years ago my eldest daughter Rasha came up with the idea of opening up Candella. We also entered the beauty business due to my three young ladies. Sisters is now expanding to four salons in Dubai alone."

Even if Shirin Abdulrazak's career now seems to be comparable to that of a Western business woman, she faced some problems of acceptance in the beginning.

"It was not smooth-sailing, it was not acceptable 25 years ago, and you had to work quietly. I remember my youngest daughter Sara when she was four years old, she was asked by her teacher: Tell me about your parents. She said: My mother is a housewife. And the teacher knew me, so when I came to school to pick up Sara, she said: I thought you work, I thought you were a businesswoman. And I said: Yes. She replied: But Sara thinks you are a housewife. So I asked Sara: Why do you think I do not work? And she said: But you are always at home! The golden rule and a silent one in our house was that nothing should interfere with the welfare of the children, husband or home. Run your own business and try to keep very low key at the same time because you were not supposed to work in the first place. I used to drop the children to school, then go and do my work, then come and pick them up and go home. So the children never ever saw me working. And if they were sick I would stay at home with them – as the owner of my company, I could do that. You were not supposed to bring work home or to discuss it. Work

was for men. My husband was not supportive initially because he thought that I was just having a fling with business, this is going to end very soon – more like a hobby, he would say. Also it will take me away from my children and heavens forbid, he, the husband should come home to a house with no wife in it!! So I kept a low profile, never discussing my work or bringing files home. In fact, I made my budding business nonexistent after 2 pm. No one was ever allowed to call me from work, short of the factory burning down, lest the call disturbs my family. In those days I wore many hats and each hat had a time and place, I behaved as though my work was a 'hobby'. All said and done, looking back I can truly say that it was indeed my wonderful family that inspired me at every turn."

Times have changed. Over the years, Shirin Abdulrazak proved herself with her successful enterprises and her husband appreciates her sense of leadership so much that today they are partners in certain businesses. While this paved the way for her societal acceptance as a businesswoman, it also brought new pressures. Managing various businesses and a family with three children needs to be thoroughly organized. Shirin Abdukrazak managed this situation through building up teams of well educated people in her businesses that are able to steer it with or without her physical presence. Being disciplined and a team leader with well developed organizational skills are the keys to her success of balancing family and work.

"I am working with people who are better than me, more experienced, and I think that is wisdom. This is still my business, and I have full control over it, yet I can leave it for long periods of time knowing there are capable team leaders. If I had to advise the younger generation from my experience I would say wait before entering the entrepreneurial field … in a sense, young women who are newly married and want to have babies must enjoy their married life and should put their careers on a temporary back burner to simmer slowly but surely. Take four to five years off, enjoy whatever life brings to you, and rear your children so you do not have to give them to housemaids in their most formative years. Also, involve the men more. For the sake of the children and the father's bonding, it is crucial to encourage active participation between the two. Do not ever believe you are a superwoman and you can single-handedly juggle it all. It is a very lonely journey being an all powerful mommy who can do just about everything and look a perfect wife at the end of the day."

Becoming an entrepreneur is many times much harder in the beginning than starting a career by entering as an employee in someone else's company. While this is an international phenomenon, the UAE seems to offer some advantages for young motivated people who want to open up their own businesses. This is not only due to the rapid development and economic success of the country, but also due to the society's attitude of acceptance of failure in business matters.

"At the time I started, there were a number of ladies of my age group who started their business today but closed tomorrow. Dubai has had a fair share of ladies waking up one fine day and starting their own businesses, then they lost interest and it was closed down. Nobody asked them why that business failed, it just died and went to a place that all these dead businesses go to. But there are also success stories of people who failed and got up and failed and got up again."

Looking at the future, Shirin Abdulrazak thinks that the number of females in the workforce of Dubai is obviously going to increase like it has been doing for the last decade. But there is one pattern that still has to be cracked in the UAE as well as in the whole region: successful women should not only become successful leaders because of their prominent husbands or fathers, they should become successful leaders because of their own achievements and their own personality. The UAE needs entrepreneurs and in Shirin Abdulrazak's opinion the government is encouraging this wholeheartedly.

"We are probably going to see the rate of females in the workforce increasing a bit faster now. On the other hand, it is a two-pronged problem because the economic prosperity means people do not have to work by choice but by necessity. You just have to be a part of this glorious boom."

Apart from being successful, Shirin Abdulrazak wants the young generation to find out, read up, and research what is actually going on in other parts of the world.

"I want us to be innovators like we once were so many centuries ago. It is so easy to sit back and let the West export everything to us. I would want us to think out of the box and be inventors. I want to see women in particular stop following like lambs, but have a questioning mind. They should not repeat everything they hear by rote, but ask questions and make up their own opinions. Watch the media by all means, listen to your fathers' and husbands' discussions but please, think for yourself and think wisely."

On the one hand Shirin Abdulrazak is inspired by the professional achievements of her daughters. On the other hand Shirin Abdulrazak often wonders how it was possible for her mother, who approaches the age of 90 now, to do what she did 70 years ago when the problems women face today, are already quite overwhelming. If all of Mariam Behnam's achievements were possible such a long time ago, then there is no excuse for the upcoming generation's complaints about restrictions which they believe they cannot overcome.

"There is no excuse to open the door. No one is going to open it for you – you have got to open it yourself. And if the girls of the young generation do not do it, then let it be known that that is by choice. Women should start questioning issues that concern their welfare, and not be afraid to respectfully ask what can be done to bring about change. We can do this peacefully and respectfully, no need to fight for our rights or for our sisters in neighboring countries."

RASHA ABDULRAZAK-MOHEBI

Rasha Abdulrazak-Mohebi is the eldest daughter of Shirin Abdulrazak. She studied in the UAE and she is now responsible for purchasing at boutique "Candella" in Dubai, which she founded with her mother. She recently got married and now hyphenates her family name and her husband's – a current trend for young women in the UAE.

Considering the fact that her mother, Shirin Abdulrazak is a successful businesswoman in her own right, it is easy to assume that Rasha Abdulrazak-Mohebi was influenced in her decision to study and begin a professional career in business.

"I never thought that I would finish university and sit at home and do nothing. I grew up seeing my mother and other female members of my family having successful careers and busy life, and I knew that my life would be no different. In the UAE we are lucky to have our government support women in the workforce as well as being provided a good working environment."

"Emiratisation" in the UAE is a key word of the current labor market. It comprises initiatives of the government for the purpose of stimulating the employment of UAE nationals in the private sector. Within these initiatives there are also special projects dedicated to women.

"The government's support makes it easier for us to find jobs and make a career out of it. I studied at the Dubai Women's Higher Colleges of Technology and before we even graduated we were already being put into work placement to gain some experience. While I was working I felt no difference between an Emirati boy, and myself – none what so ever. We get the same salary, we get the same treatment, and we get the same opportunities, if not more."

Rasha Abdulrazak-Mohebi also feels that most of the newly married couples nowadays consist of both a working man and a working woman.

"I think the majority of men especially today with the rising costs, actually like their women to work and have their own financial independence."

In Rasha Abdulrazak-Mohebi's personal life plan there are still other priorities before working. While she does not feel that somebody else forces her to live a certain life she prefers to concentrate on her family in the future.

"My first priority will always be my husband and my children. The only thing to stop me from a career would be me. It would be my own choice – either because I do not feel ready for it or maybe because I want to spend more time with my children until they are older. I have discussed my career with my husband, and he has always been very supportive. He understands that I need to work and contribute to society. I am lucky to be married to someone who understands it. My mother and grandmother did not have an easy time entering the workforce and had to fight for it. Just hearing about their struggles makes me more determined to work hard and take nothing for granted."

Openness and freedom are also the basic principles that Rasha Abdulrazak-Mohebi would follow when bringing up her future children, especially her future daughters.

"I would bring them up the very same way that I have been brought up: with trust, good education, good understanding of the world around us, the ability to adjust into different cultures and not to be narrow-minded. I would prefer my daughters to have a career and be financially independent. Whatever she decides and wherever her interests take her, my husband and I will support her."

MARYAM AL MURSHEDI AL SHEHI

Maryam Al Murshedi Al Shehi holds the position of the Deputy Director General at Ras Al Khaimah Free Trade Zone Authority (RAK FTZA). She obtained a degree of Higher Diploma in Business Information from the Higher Colleges of Technology as well as Higher National Diploma from Business and Technical Educational Council in United Arab Emirates in Information Management. On her way she was especially supported by her mother and steadily looked up at two leaders of her country.

"My mother is my number one supporter. She always knew what I can be and has always encouraged me to reach my full potential. She is the one who gives me courage and tells me to do more because she knows I can. My mother is the one who gave me trust to pursue my dream and the confidence to achieve it. Furthermore, I have two role models: His Highness Sheikh Zayed Bin Sultan Al Nahyan for his wisdom and his support to empower UAE women. His wisdom is what drove this country to where it us now. My other role model is His Highness Sheikh

Mohammed Bin Rashid Al Maktoum for his ambition and vision. It is through his vision that Dubai is what it is now by overseeing the development initiating several world-class projects that put the country in the international attention. His drive and ambition is incomparable."

Maryam Al Murshedi Al Shehi joined the Ras Al Khaimah Free Trade Zone Authority in 1998 right after her graduation in the Administration Department, and quickly and steadily made her way to the top management of the RAK FTZA organisation. Asking her which skills she considers to be important for leadership, she answers:

"I consider drive and ambition very important for women in leadership. Decision making and independence is also important. Women are always considered emotional but I think a combination of emotion and practicality is what gives us an edge over the men in general. A little emotion to guide you with your decision and 90% practicality is very important. For both women and men I think that talent, personality and character are very important characteristics, if you believe in yourself you can achieve anything."

Thinking about the women's role in the society of the UAE Maryam Al Murshedi Al Shehi concludes:

"Already in the earlier years Arab women has been known to own their own businesses and have financial means. It has evolved and has become more in the spotlight in the recent years because women are becoming more prominent in the business and the society. Women are more ambitious now than before and have bigger aspirations for themselves. Women must not be satisfied with the status quo and be committed to what they believe in. The society focus is changing, and with the support and acceptance it is enabling more women to strive for more and achieve their aspirations."

Maryam Al Murshedi Al Shehi loves her work and the drive to excel and is proud of what she has accomplished. She has always been revered for her inspirational and tireless dedication to the improvement, advancement and development of the organisation by women and men likewise.

"I do not see any difference with working with male subordinates as I do not capitalise on being a woman to achieve what I want. It is a business environment and I believe everyone is equal – gender has nothing to do with your capabilities. I work hard as anyone else and I fight to have my ideas taken seriously not because I am a woman but because it is a worthwhile one. I do not give them the opportunity to treat me differently otherwise."

Maryam Al Murshedi Al Shehi‘s understanding of equality is also applicable for a comparison of Western business women and UAE business women:

"There is not a big difference between the two. The channels might be different but because of globalisation everything is changing for the better and the gaps between these differences are becoming closer. The differences can be taken in a positive light too as it can be a learning curve for one another. Exchanging different ideas is not a bad thing; it can help forge a better communication. Both are finding ways to communicate with each other and having an open exchange of ideas helps breach these gaps. At the end of the day, we are all working for the same purpose; we are all driven by ambition and trying to get to where we all want to be."

REEMA ABBAS

Reema Abbas is a professional artist concentrating on modern abstract artworks often using the human form as the main subject matter. She gets her inspiration from various people around the corner and around the world. If she sees people doing something extraordinarily or if she reads about someone pursuing his dreams – that creates her inspiration. All of this leads her to the main message in her artworks: that people should concentrate on the things that bring them together rather than the things that set them apart.

"Creativity is a vital tool to help us bring everyone together with a message of peace and love."

Reema Abbas was born in Al Ain in 1974 and later on moved to Sharjah together with her two sisters, a brother, her mother and father. She describes herself as a more introverted person during her childhood.

"I did not like mixing up with the crowd. I felt that I was different. I had different ideas in my head. So I used to go to the art room to escape from the kids. A lot of my time I spend in the art room developing my art and practicing drawing. So a lot of my childhood memories from school are from the art room."

After finishing high school at the age of seventeen she went to the UK where her personality quickly developed to become more confident and open while living alone abroad. Her mother and father, both educated in the UK, never hesitated to send their children abroad for education – it was more a necessity for them to go. Even her extended family was mostly educated abroad. So the way was paved for Reema Abbas to follow her passion internationally and she went to acquire a B-Tech Diploma in "Fine Arts and Design" as well as a Fashion Design & Marketing Degree in London.

"I really enjoyed living in the UK, because I could explore my artistic flair there more. There was a lot of inspiration for me because of all the museums and galleries, very artistic people with nothing holding them back really. I was glad to experience that there. And I came back with still the same ideals that I learnt at Art College and Fashion College. I am trying to keep on with the same vision as they told us there. That's why you see me a bit different. You have to be open-minded as an artist. You cannot have anything holding you back, because that would defect your artistic integrity."

Reema Abbas returned to the UAE in her twenties. At this time working as an artist in the country was difficult because of a small art movement and very few art galleries. It was not an unusual thing for women to get into art but it was unacceptable for art to show certain figures and scenes in public. These are cultural limitations that artists have to abide by. On the other hand life in the UAE offered much inspiration due to the people with their traditions and values, the beauty of the nature, the sea and the desert and last but not least the fast changing environment. The change is very valuable for Reema Abbas because it brings opportunities which were not there before for men, for women and for art.

However, time was not yet right for a young artist to take off in the UAE and Reema Abbas decided to start to work as a trainer for a large cosmetic chain for her first professional years. Soon she discovered that this was not what she satisfied and she felt that she had to move on and build up her own art business.

"It was scary in the beginning though. I just thought I have to be determined and do it, because no one else is going to do it for me, if I am not doing the first step. You always have fear when you have an idea. If you want to do something for yourself there are always barriers. But you have to go over these barriers. I noticed that a lot of people try to stop here. I had a lot of people saying, how can you make it as an artist, and really pay the bills? I just thought that many people are doing it and I believe I can do it. I have the skills, I have the talent and I have the determination."

Until today it is not an easy living as a young artist in the UAE. To become more known and exposed in their profession young artists especially face the problem of a missing voice in public. On the one hand the few existing galleries in the country prefer to exhibit established artists and on the other hand opening up your own gallery is almost a pioneer work.

"If I have my own gallery in the future, I will encourage up-coming artists, because you do find energy in their paintings which is amazing. Currently the possibilities in other galleries are very limited which is a bit frustrating. But I am not going to let this stop me from having my art distributed all over the UAE. And I also want to go international with my art in the long run."

Comparing conditions of life for women in the UAE between past generations and the generation of Reema Abbas is impressive as the story of her life tells. Emirati women now go internationally alone and at a very young age, they get involved into most professions and they follow their own path. In fact, women of the young generations are now finding it unchallenging to stay at home and not to contribute to the society. The two preconditions for them to get involved in a professional life are the feeling for a need to work and an open-minded husband and family. Some women do not work because of financial comfort but they still have the wish to invest in businesses and get active in this way. Men remain to have the upper hand and are the primary decision makers but today there is a growing number of husbands and fathers who let their daughters live their lives and explore their opportunities and now it's absolutely common as we see more and more women contributing to the UAE's growing economy.

Projects lead by women for women

During the last decades a number of projects were initiated to support women in many aspects of their lives and to strengthen their role in the society. It started with gatherings of women and based on that the foundation of formal women's councils in the seventies and eighties of the last century. It went on with the evolvement of successful business women as role models in the nineties. And finally it reached a level where many women are well educated and they are an integral part of the daily business live in the United Arab Emirates. Nowadays they lead teams or even whole companies, they make far-reaching decisions in politics and they represent their country to the outside world.

Looking back, it was the First Lady who initiated programs exclusively for women in her country. The President's wife H. H. Sheikha Fatima bint Mubarak founded the first women's society in the country in 1972, the Abu Dhabi Women's Society. It was followed by initiatives of the other emirates – the Dubai Women's Development Society, the Sharjah Women's Development Society, the Umm al-Mou'meneen Women's Development Society in Ajman, the Umm al-Qaiwain Development Society and the Ras al-Khaimah Women's Development Society emerged. These societies were subsequently linked together under the UAE Women's Federation which was established in 1975, again headed by H. H. Sheikha Fatima. The UAE Women's Federation is an autonomous body with its own budget. It has a number of committees to run its activities, such as religious affairs, mother and child care, social affairs, cultural affairs, sports, heritage and the arts. Committees formed within this organisation established a variety of women's activities. These committees include those dedicated to religious affairs, childcare, social affairs, cultural affairs, sports, heritage and the arts. Some of their activities include running nurseries and kindergartens thus permitting mothers to go out to work. Other activities include the dissemination of nutritional information for pregnant women and new mothers, a United Nations Development Programme for reviving the close association of some of the country's women with the land, classes for tailoring, embroidery and housekeeping, missions to rural areas and mothering and childcare classes supported by UNICEF. Furthermore, they facilitate the free borrowing of library books, an activity that has indicated rising levels of social and literary consciousness in areas formally of high illiteracy, according to the United Nations. Depending on the geographical size of the emirate, the individual societies may have more than one branch and there are now a total of 31 branches of the six societies. The goal of these establishments is to raise women's spiritual, cultural and social standards and therewith enable them to contribute to their countries development guided by the instructions and values of the Islamic religion. They built the platform for communication and activity of women and they pay special attention to women's education. One of their important tasks in its beginnings was an adult literacy programme which was one reason for female literacy rates soon matching those of males. The Federation is also engaged in health, education and social campaigns to raise the standard of living of UAE families.

Connected to the chambers of commerce and industry in the various emirates, business women councils evolved. The Abu Dhabi Businesswomen Council and the Dubai Businesswomen Council commenced its formal activities in 2002 and support its members since then with information, networking opportunities, seminars, lectures, workshops and exhibitions. The current president of the Dubai Businesswomen Council, Raja Al Gurg, is also one of the most prominent female business leaders in the UAE. The former prize-winning headmistress worked her way up through her father's company until she was chosen over her brothers to become head of the Easa Saleh Al Gurg Group of Companies, one of the leading groups in the UAE. She also serves as board member of the Dubai Chamber and the Emirates Business Women Council. Raja Al Gurg strongly promotes and encourages young women to become active business leaders.

The Mohammed Bin Rashid Establishment for Young Business Leaders founded in 2002 in Dubai is another establishment that was initiated by the leaders of the country and that pays special attention to women. It focuses on entrepreneurship and assists both women and men to become successful entrepreneurs. According to them research makes it clear that there is a considerable number of Emirati women who are involved in small-scale economic activities. Both traditional activities (e. g. perfume mixing, traditional cloth making and various handicrafts) and modern activities (e. g. advanced information and communication techniques and up-to-date business practices) belong to the important basis for a healthy economy and are carried out by women.

The organization Women in Technology UAE (WIT UAE) aims to empower women and expand their participation in the workforce by providing curricula and training opportunities in business planning, professional development and information technology (IT). The establishment is funded by the Middle East Partnership Initiative (MEPI) of the U.S. Department of State, managed by the Institute of International Education (IIE) West Coast Center, and implemented in collaboration with partners in the UAE. The organization believes that acquiring hard skills, especially in the field of information technology, is a powerful building block for individuals and organizations to empower women to play an integral role in shaping their country's future.

In 2007 a company named Forsa was founded in Dubai – the first of its kind to provide investment opportunities exclusively for women in the UAE and GCC region. Forsa offers its clients the opportunity to invest in the region's booming economic development and to empower them to realize their business aspirations by providing access to professional expertise and support. The company's aim is to provide tailor-made financial advice to women as well as start-up investments for businesses led by Emirati women.

Women are also focused when it comes to awarding exceptional commitment, skills or talents. The yearly Emirates Businesswomen Award launched by Shell in 2003 in association with Dubai Quality Group, is aimed at publicly acknowledging and rewarding the contribution of businesswomen (National & Expatriates) in the UAE, by identifying and recognising outstanding business prowess. Furthermore the aim is to inspire the future generation of women to achieve their full potential and maximise their contribution to UAE's economy. The criterion for the award include: leadership skills; future goals and performance; business, professional and career achievements; community contributions and participation; and innovation.

Business women in the UAE are encouraged to apply either for the "business owner category" or the "professional category". Beside the reputation for the women themselves and their businesses and projects, the opportunity to network with other women achievers from various fields is an important motivation for women to apply for the award. Furthermore the organizers offer individual feedback and coaching sessions to the applicants which might boost the business women's career even further. Award winners in 2007 included Maryam Al Bannah, General Manager Corporate Support Services at Dubai World Trade Centre, and Lama Farsakh, Vice President & Resident Manager of Engineering Consultant Group. In 2006

Nafisa Al Mulla, head and owner of Al Murooj English School, Sharjah and Rania Abdallah, Regional Human Resources Manager for Middle East, Asia and Africa at PepsiCo International, Dubai were awarded.

CONCLUDING REMARKS

A widely recognised leadership trait is the ability to remain composed and calm in crisis situations. Feminine leadership styles are not better or worse than the traditional male-oriented ones, they are just different. Researchers have observed that when compared to men, women are likely to surpass the latter in collective decision making and other constructive leadership skills. As examples of appointments of women in politics, the judicial system and business show in this book, the UAE is on its way to benefit from women's leadership skills.

However there are numerous myths that are associated with the role of women in organisations. Although stereotyping of women has been around through history and many are untrue, it is particularly interesting that many of these characteristics are actually attributes in the knowledge-based economy. For example, it is often said that women are naturally too emotional for business decision making. In fact, emotion and more specifically "emotional intelligence" is highly desirable in the knowledge-based economy and assists in decision making particularly in aspects of human resources.

Criticism, particularly in the Middle East is that a woman's role as mother and housewife would be impossible if she were to take on an additional role outside the domestic arena. However, these judgements are being proved wrong by the growing number of energetic young women in the region who are proving that a balanced life is possible, together with growth in western-style day-care centres in addition to centralised family support.

The growing contributions of women in the UAE's industrial market and their strides towards managerial positions have transformed the conventional definition of a leader. In transformational leadership theory, women are inspired and motivationally driven to assume this leadership style. Leadership styles adopted by women in the corporate world are both democratic and participative. And though many may believe that gender is a determining factor to effective leadership, it remains that main divider in leadership styles is objective selection of qualified candidates.

The traditional preconception about prohibiting women from work has changed as now the percentage of women in the labour market is more than the men. The performance of women in the labour market is much more excellent. Not only this, women excelled in education and in different fields that made them enter the labour force in higher rates.

The emphasis on diversification, advances in education, Emiratisation and change in social status are catalysts for encouraging women to recognize and apply their potential as professionals and leaders. Emirati women have made a window into the glass ceiling and are walking stride in stride with their male counterparts setting new standards.

About the Authors

Kristin Augsburg: Spent five years in the UAE; four of which working with the German Industry and Commerce Office in Dubai. Editor of the "Geschäftshandbuch VAE" ('Business Guide UAE', a publication of the German Industry and Commerce Office, distributed in Germany through the German Office for Foreign Trade, May 2005).

MMag. Isabell A. Claus: Former Assistant to the CEO & President of DaimlerChrysler Middle East FZE in Dubai. Educated in International Business, Business and Law as well as Arabic Studies at Vienna University of Economics and Business, Vienna University, Harvard University, London School of Economics and Dubai University College. Specialized in economic and social research topics related to the countries of the Gulf Cooperation Council (GCC). Several academic and non-academic publications as well as lectures internationally on leadership, strategy and the development of the GCC countries and their institutions.

Dr. Kasim Randeree BEng(Hons), MA, PhD: Academic background includes Research Fellow at the University of Oxford; Visiting Lecturer at The University of Manchester; Lecturer at The British University in Dubai, United Arab Emirates University and University of Lincoln; Adjunct Professor at the American University in Dubai and Assistant Lecturer at the University of Hull. Over 100 published articles in international journals and conferences and editorial responsibilities with five international publications. Research interests in leadership, organisation studies, project management, Emiratisation, the role of Emirati women, multiculturalism and diversity in the Arabian Gulf region, the advancement of education in the Middle East and Islamic perspectives on leadership and management.

Wirtschaft: Forschung und Wissenschaft

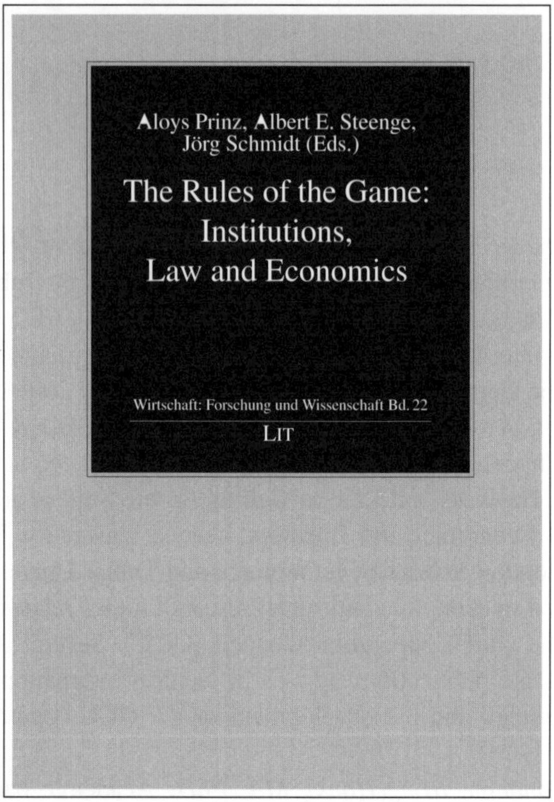

Aloys Prinz; Albert E. Steenge; Jörg Schmidt (Eds.)
The Rules of the Game: Institutions, Law and Economics
In a global economy, environmental challenges and present as well as future demand and supply of energy are of crucial importance. Rules and institutions here are general tools to provide guidance for welfare improving solutions. In this context, researchers of the School of Management and Governance of the University of Twente and the Institute of Public Economics of the University of Muenster presented papers at a seminar at Rothenberge, published in this volume. The three main topics are: economic and institutional aspects of energy markets, economic implications of environmental laws, and the economics of international trade and markets.
Bd. 22, 2007, 224 S., 54,90 €, br., ISBN 978-3-8258-0693-4

INFER Research Perspectives
edited by Michael Pickhardt

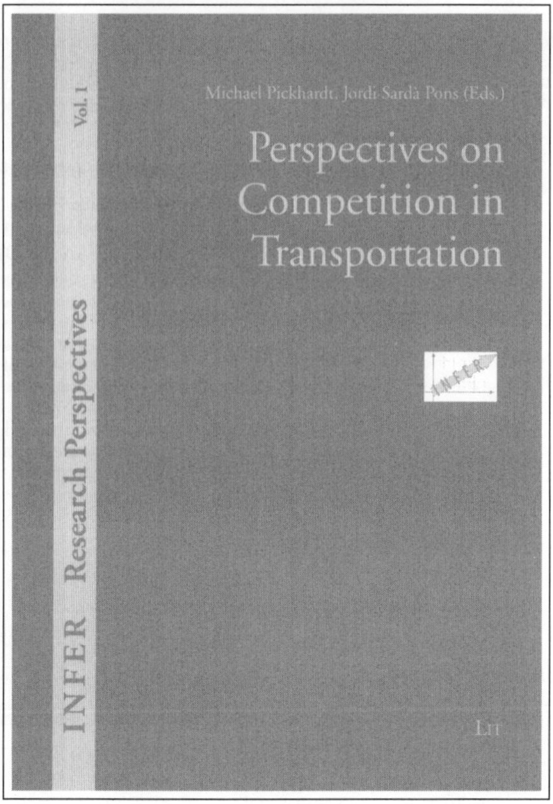

Michael Pickhardt; Jordi Sardà Pons (Eds.)
Perspectives on Competition in Transportation
Issues of competition seem to have been neglected for a long time in the transportation sector. But the provision of transport services at competitive prices and quantities may have an important impact on economic development, both from a regional and a global perspective. This volume addresses such issues of competition in transportation. Part I deals with the air transport sector, part II is concerned with the road transport sector, part III takes a look at transportation costs and, in the final part, some visions of competition in transportation are discussed.
Bd. 1, 2006, 256 S., 49,90 €, br., ISBN 3-8258-9670-6

LIT Verlag Berlin – Münster – Wien – Zürich – London
Auslieferung Deutschland / Österreich / Schweiz: siehe Impressumsseite

Henrik Egbert; Clemens Esser (Eds.)
Migration and Labour Markets in the Social Sciences
The interplay of migration and labour markets is a phenomenon too diverse to be explained by a single theory. Thus, this volume, based on contributions presented during a workshop in Saarbrücken, Germany, brings together experts in migration research from economics, political science, and sociology. The rationale for choosing the topic is the existence of misconceptions and prejudices in public debate about migration. The contributions investigate the main effects of migration on labour markets for both, the home and the host country, and discuss normative, positive, and instrumental aspects of migration from different perspectives.
Bd. 2, 2007, 112 S., 29,90 €, br., ISBN 978-3-8258-0229-5

Frank Fichert; Justus Haucap;
Kai Rommel (Eds.)
Competition Policy in Network Industries
The promotion of competition in Europe's network industries has been in the foreground of economic policy in recent years. Network industries have undergone dramatic changes, involving privatisation, liberalisation and de- as well as re-regulation. But there are still many unresolved problems in both economic policy as well as economic research. Hence, a vivid exchange between academics and policy makers has emerged to find the optimal framework for these industries. This volume contributes to this discussion, containing several papers on various network industries.
Bd. 3, 2007, 304 S., 49,90 €, br., ISBN 978-3-8258-0231-8

LIT Verlag Berlin – Münster – Wien – Zürich – London
Auslieferung Deutschland / Österreich / Schweiz: siehe Impressumsseite

Helena Marques; Elias Soukiazis; Pedro Cerqueira (Eds.)

Perspectives on Integration and Globalisation

Problems of integration and globalisation and the implications of such processes on individual countries have been on the spotlight of the economic debate among economists and politicians over the last decade. Both developed and developing countries are involved in the processes of trade and capital liberalisation, with the extent of gain or loss depending on their ability to explore the newly arising opportunities and to adapt their economies to the new international environment. This volume analyses some of these challenges brought by the movements towards a higher regional integration and higher international interdependency.

Bd. 7, 2008, 272 S., 49,90 €, br., ISBN 978-3-8258-1545-5

Christian Richter (Ed.)

Bounded Rationality in Economics and Finance

The dominant hypothesis in mainstream economics is the assumption of prefect rationality. However, there are two dilemmas: Whenever this assumption was used empirical evidence turned out to be against it. Secondly, this assumption is far from reality, for example, because individuals usually do not possess all relevant information. Therefore, this volume addresses issues of bounded rationality in different areas. The first part investigates bounded rationality in financial markets, the second part investigates the effects of bounded rationality on industrial organizations and the third part deals with bounded rationality in price theory, environmental economics and public management.

Bd. 8, 2008, 200 S., 39,90 €, br., ISBN 978-3-8258-1614-8

LIT Verlag Berlin – Münster – Wien – Zürich – London
Auslieferung Deutschland / Österreich / Schweiz: siehe Impressumsseite

Edward Shinnick (Ed.)
Public Finance, Monetary Policy and Market Issues
Economies throughout both the developed and developing world are interconnected like never before, whether it is the financing of global challenges, monetary integration among a group of countries or trade across national borders. This increasing degree of interconnection brings both opportunities and challenges for the countries involved. This volume provides an analysis of three distinct but closely related themes of economic interconnection: Public Finance, Monetary Policy and Market Issues. We hope this collection of papers will stimulate further debate on these issues and in doing so will help to broaden the exchange of ideas among economists in both academia and business.
Bd. 5, 2009, 368 S., 69,90 €, br., ISBN 978-3-8258-1544-8

Transnational and Transatlantic American Studies

edited by Mita Banerjee (Siegen), Kornelia Freitag (Bochum), Walter Grünzweig (Dortmund), Randi Gunzenhäuser (Dortmund), Wilfried Raussert (Bielefeld), Michael Wala (Bochum)

Kevin Cahill; Lene Johannessen (Eds.)
Considering Class
Essays on the Discourse of the American Dream
In the 21st century hardly any aspects of human existence are left unexplored by postmodern theories and discourses of subjectivity and individuality, of hybridity and identity, of race, gender and ethnicity. Conspicuous, however, among these critical inquiries is the relatively little attention devoted to the category of class. This absence is particularly alarming at a time when neo-liberalism and post-capitalism feed on cultural fragmentation and ideological relativism. The contributions in *Considering Class: Essays on the Discourse of the American Dream* address the (dys)functional position of class in American socio-political and cultural reality from a variety of disciplinary perspectives. While it is open to debate whether class is more resistant to being relativized than other categories, there is increasing recognition that class remains a critical category with the potential to transcend the rifts and divisions that run along lines of race, ethnicity and gender, and with the potential to reconfigure the current American political landscape.
Bd. 4, 2007, 224 S., 29,90 €, br., ISBN 978-3-8258-0259-2

Frauenstudien und emanzipatorische Frauenarbeit

hrsg. von Irmhild Kettschau und Elisabeth de Sotelo

Elisabeth de Sotelo (Ed.)
New Women of Spain
Social-Political and Philosophical Studies of Feminist Thought
This collection of essays provides an insight into the status of feminist positions among female Spanish scholars. The focus is placed on the social and political achievements that feminism has attained since the transition to democracy in Spain. It gives an outline of the radical changes in the image of women. Above all, however, this reader illustrates the extent of academic research on feminist issues which has developed and become increasingly differentiated over the past 30 years. This book is a dramatic example of the explosive development of feminism and the new status of women in Spain.
Bd. 4, 2005, 464 S., 25,90 €, br., ISBN 3-8258-6199-6